D1484891

50 DESIGNERS

50 COSTUMES

CONCEPT TO CHARACTER

Academy of Motion Picture Arts and Sciences

Published on the occasion of the exhibition

**"Fifty Designers/Fifty Costumes:
Concept to Character"**

at the Galleries of
The Academy of Motion Picture Arts and Sciences
Beverly Hills, California
September 10 – December 5, 2004

Presented in association with the Costume Designers Guild

Front cover:
Detail of fabric designed by Judianna Makovsky
for Richard Harris as Albus Dumbledore in
HARRY POTTER AND THE SORCERER'S STONE (2001).

TABLE OF CONTENTS

FOREWORD

Jeffrey Kurland
Governor, The Academy of Motion Picture Arts and Sciences
2004

Throughout my career, I have had the pleasure and privilege to design costumes for a wide variety of films spanning all periods, for a great many wonderful directors and actors. This alchemy of past, present and future, along with the collaboration of incredibly talented and esoteric artists, in front of and behind the camera, is what makes costume design one of the most integral and special of the cinematic arts.

Concept, character and color are the basis of costume design. All costume designs, be they period, contemporary or fantasy, have their roots in these basic tenets. The costume designers and their work seen in this exhibition run the gamut of design and style from A to Z. But even with these artistic variances they are all true to the same goal: to tell a story through characters, created with a nod to reality, imagination and wit.

Costumes are not mere garments. They are visual tools used to release the soul of a character – a way to lift a character off the page and into a three dimensional world. Costume design is one of three departments responsible for creating the visuals of a film. Along with the production designer and cinematographer, costume designers create a visual structure that houses the characters a writer has created within the concept the director has laid out. In close partnership with actor and director, the costume designer helps to tell the story before words are even uttered. Costumes dominate the foreground action throughout a film, shaping the characters and thus helping to move the story forward with what one could describe as the visual narrative.

Since the first films were created at the beginning of the 20th century, costumes were an important part of the filmmaking process. The names Rambova, Banton, Plunkett, Head, Jeakins and Rose to name a few, are recognized for their contribution to cinema through the specific art of costume design. When we think of iconic films, we picture the actors in costume, because much of the film's beauty, grandeur and superior storytelling is due in great part to the art of costume design. In 1948, the Academy of Motion Picture Arts and Sciences wisely recognized the art of costume design with its own Oscar. We are the unsung heroes of character development, the pioneers of disguising art as the ordinary.

Costume design has many artistic faces. Period costumes are the most noticeable and seemingly most spectacular of the art form. With the designer's eye and imagination, in conjunction with copious historical research, these costumes beautifully recreate a time gone by. Consider the art of designing contemporary costumes, less obvious and showy. With subtlety and nuance, these designs represent a shrewd observation of contemporary society and enhance a film and the characters that people it in an almost invisible way. These all too often ignored artistic offerings are exhibited here alongside their grander and more attention-getting cousins. They all bear the mark of hard work, talent and devotion to creating great cinema.

This exhibition celebrates a new generation of costume designers who are as talented, imaginative and devoted to quality as their renowned predecessors. With greater time restraints and more budgetary demands, creativity still flourishes. I hope that you will enjoy this exhibition displaying the art of costume design, and come to a new understanding of its importance in the filmmaking process.

INTRODUCTION

"CHARACTER COMES FIRST"

Deborah Nadoolman Landis, PhD
President, The Costume Designers Guild, Local 892
2004

COSTUME DESIGN IS STORYTELLING

The intention of this exhibition is to illuminate the costume design process, which begins with a script and ends on the last day of shooting. On display is a broad sampling of work by an international community of costume designers, covering the last five years of film releases. Today's movies mix the old cinema traditions of glamour and romanticism with new wave realism and twenty-first century cross-cultural pollination. As evidenced by the costumes in the exhibition, film design is approached with a greater emphasis on accuracy and faithfulness to the script than ever before. As we celebrate the achievements of costume designers, we also aim to dispel some common myths and misperceptions about the craft.

At the root of the problem is a pervasive uncertainty about the very purpose of costume design. Film costumes serve two equal purposes: to support the narrative by creating memorable characters, and to provide balance within the frame by using color, texture and silhouette. Costume and production design are the yin and yang of film design and are equally legitimate. Costume designers are skilled professionals trained to work in the two-dimensional format of the film frame, and costumes are designed to appear on one actor, on one set, lit and framed in the most specific way. All clothing used in a fictional film is considered costume, enriched by a magnified theatrical scale, through which a heightened reality is utilized to reveal the nature of each character.

Costumes are one of the tools a film director has to tell a story. Milena Canonero creates "costumes that are in harmony with the director's concept of the movie." Costumes provide essential information to the audience. Our attention is focused on that which the director chooses to reveal to us: a close-up may emphasize or reveal details – a cuff, a lapel or a collar – for a deliberate narrative purpose. Costumes are so much more than clothes – costumes embody the psychological, social and emotional condition of the character at a particular moment in the script. Anthony Powell sums it up when he declares, "It is impossible for me to design for the actor unless I know who the character is." Costume allows audiences to recognize characters before the actor delivers the dialogue. Faced with the non-linear structure of BIG FISH, designer Colleen Atwood created visual shorthand because she had "so much to reveal in small cinematic moments…" Simply put, a costume designer strives to conceptualize and design garments that capture and define the personalities of fictional characters in a screenplay.

Accomplished actors often discover their character in the fitting room. After many discussions with Daniel Day Lewis, Sandy Powell was able to communicate her vision for GANGS OF NEW YORK only after Daniel arrived for his first fitting. The minute he put the costumes on "he said he could see the character." When Johnny Depp insisted to Penny Rose that of the six pirate hats lying on the floor of the fitting room, "there was only one hat…that was [Jack Sparrow's] hat," she made twelve more exact copies for PIRATES OF THE CARIBBEAN. Julie Weiss explains that usually the costume designer shares in the creation of fictional characters in the fitting room "but Salma Hayek had wanted to do Frida [Kahlo] for so long that she didn't realize when she actually became Frida.

THE RESEARCH PROCESS

Great costumes are the result of astute observation, analysis and imagination. Research is required regardless of whether the project is period or modern. The time available to conduct this critical research can vary, contingent on the nature of the production and its budget. Designers are inspired by paintings and sculpture, literature, photography, nature, music, childhood memories, other movies, other designers and freely associating all of these. Often, pressed for time, they do not have the luxury to internalize and reflect upon these insights. Gabriella Pescucci channeled pre-Raphaelite paintings for the romantic costumes in A MIDSUMMER NIGHT'S DREAM, while Betsy Heimann evoked the lyrics of a Jimi Hendrix ballad as inspiration for Kate Hudson's "band aide" in ALMOST FAMOUS. Each project presents unique research and design opportunities for the designer.

As a result of their intense research, costume designers compile a scrapbook of photos, family albums, home movies, yearbooks, hair and make-up styles, sketches, fabric swatches, and virtually any visual reference they can acquire. This research volume acts as a "bible" for costume designers. The bible is shared with all creative collaborators – the director, actor, cinematographer, production designer and with hair and make up. The costume designer will also use the bible as the centerpiece of discussions with the costume crew.

Infinitely resourceful, today's costume designers utilize new technologies and unconventional solutions to challenges presented by the script, often under the added pressure of having no time and little budget. Costumes need to be practical while also using cutting-edge techniques; fabrics and paints (some never used on garments before) can be employed to achieve the desired look on film. Working in subfreezing temperatures on EXTREME OPS, Maria Schiker needed to "keep the actors warm and dry" in lightweight ski clothes that were also attractive. For the horrific warping and melting of a thermal suit in THE CORE, Dan Lester became an expert in a technically advanced fabric called "asteroid," and Mona May conducted endless experiments and camera tests with reflective glass powder "to find the right effect" for the shimmering ghosts in Haunted Mansion.

PERIOD VS. MODERN: WHAT DEFINES COSTUME DESIGN?

Costume design in a modern film is often required to be invisible. Contemporary costumes are considered successful if audiences DON'T notice the costumes at all, but if they are nonetheless deeply connected to the characters. Ellen Mirojnick contends that designing a contemporary film means that "you have to work doubly hard to make them [the costumes] disappear…" In FIGHT CLUB, Michael Kaplan explains that his "job was to produce clothes that looked like they came from thrift shops…clothes that nobody would want." Kristin Burke believes that the audience "will not consciously perceive [Bill Macy's] costume changes" in THE COOLER, "but will be affected by them." Drama does not have the corner on psychological character analysis. For the comedy A MIGHTY WIND, Durinda Wood's costumes embraced "all of the humorous oddities of real life."

Costume designers consider modern films to be as complex as any lavish period project. However, like the popular myth of actors improvising their dialogue, modern costumes – everyday clothes – are taken for granted by the public and the press. Since everyone gets dressed in the morning, everyone considers themselves an expert on contemporary clothes. As Joanna Johnston puts it, "Contemporary films depend on delicate and subtle design; it's a very fine line. The designers can go too far, or you can understate it and not make the point. The audience must be able to say, absolutely, 'I recognize that person.'" The hunt for accurate costumes in a romantic comedy or drama may lead a designer to an airport, hospital or for lunch at the Conde Nast commissary when the subject is a young fashion editor, as in HOW TO LOSE A GUY IN 10 DAYS. Nothing that appears on screen is casual – every accessory and costume is a deliberate choice made by a designer.

All motion pictures today utilize a combination of bought, rented and manufactured costumes. The idea that modern costumes are "shopped" by designers, reaching the screen unaltered, with fashion designers' labels intact, is a common falsehood. POSSESSION made use of both period and contemporary costumes. Jenny Beavan "refitted, dyed and customized" every purchased or rented costume in that film, then her challenge was "to mix them up and make the labels disappear." Jacqueline West, designer of QUILLS, explains, "It's about getting toward the center of the character and finding out what that person is…whether you make the clothes for them or shop for them. To me it's more limiting doing contemporary movies…your choices are just based upon…what [the character's] choices would be."

PAINTING THE FRAME: COLOR, TEXTURE & SILHOUETTE

Costumes provide color, silhouette, balance and symmetry to the film frame. Because they are worn by the actors, costumes dominate the foreground action, providing a resting place for our eyes. Each frame of film provides a proscenium for foreground and background action; cinematographers, production designers and costume designers collaborate to fill those rectangular dimensions as authoritatively as in a conventional theater. This team of artists works together to paint and light each frame of film as meticulously as a canvas, designing and engineering the invented universe of the script as interpreted by the director. They make the world – and the characters that people it – come alive.

For the design of HARRY POTTER, Judianna Makovsky worked intimately with the production designer to keep Harry's world "elegant, simple, clean and a little silly." To bring the filmmakers' vision to screen, these artists must also deliberate on the overall mood and color palette for the film. Color is a powerful tool used to underscore the narrative and create a cohesive fictional space. The dialogue may be the melody of a movie, but color provides the harmony. And it's important to have a strong reference point from which to create a style. For THE LAST SAMURAI Ngila Dickson determined that "each character could be very much identified by the color of their costume." Using exactly the same technique for the modern romantic comedy HOW TO LOSE A GUY IN 10 DAYS, Karen Patch neutralized the cocktail party atmosphere "so that Kate [Hudson] would stand out in that room." To ease audience confusion in the tragic Armenian saga ARARAT, Beth Pasternak crafted "a limited palette to identify [ethnic] groups."

Undergarments are hidden from the audience but play a traditional role in helping actors find their character. Corseting alters an actor's gait, posture, and delivery while providing a distinct and readily identifiable silhouette. Three recent Victorian dramas used this to great effect. For his gender-bending role in NICHOLAS NICKLEBY, Ruth Myers bound Barry Humphries' waist for a period gown "based on a specific corset." Carol Ramsey confided, "The director …really felt [the corset] was the key to [Winnie's] character" in TUCK EVERLASTING. Once Ann Roth "got Nicole Kidman in that corset, and her waistline down to 23 inches, [Nicole] was overwhelmed" with the Civil War hourglass silhouette for COLD MOUNTAIN. By contrast, shape also was a starting point for the very goofy super-spy Austin Powers. Deena Appel decided early on that Austin required a "recognizably signature silhouette." When Charlie Chaplin's Tramp or Indiana Jones is recognizable simply by his iconic shadow, it testifies to the power of costume in silhouette.

FASHION VS. COSTUME

A word about fashion. Fashion is a visual art of enormous creativity. Fashion is about commerce, change, comfort, individuality and standing out in a crowd – or conformity and the status quo. It's easy for the public to confuse actors with the characters they play. The red carpet phenomenon exemplifies this fusion of fact and fantasy, role and reality. In a celebrity-obsessed media, celebrity and stardom eclipse the serious endeavor of creating authentic fictional characters. Not every costume is meant to make a glamorous entrance. As designer Abigail Murray notes, "Characters are not about fashion. Characters are about real life." Fashion and costume are not synonymous; they are antithetical. They have directly opposing and contradictory purposes.

Costumes are never clothes. Unlike fashion, which is designed for our three-dimensional world, costumes are designed to appear in two dimensions on film, which flattens and distorts the image. What's pretty in person may not be pretty on screen, needing the enhancement of color, texture or silhouette to "read" on camera. Costumes are part of the visual jigsaw puzzle that is the frame – and designers consider the entire picture when they design a costume. Floral wallpaper, burgundy herringbone upholstery – even the turquoise of the BMW the actor is driving – are entered into the design equation. Expensive clothes feel fabulous. Costumes don't have to feel good; they just have to look like they feel good on screen. Costumes don't have to be expensive; they just have to look expensive in the movie. Fashion designers often credit classic and current movies as influencing their style. But they are inspired by the costume design – the irresistible elixir of fascinating characters and a story well told.

MASTERS OF THEIR CRAFT

Collapsed production time and ever shortened schedules present nightmares for costume designers, and they are veterans of overcoming obstacles. Trained never to say "no," designers really believe they can deliver a miracle on request – and most of the time they can. Workdays can run over sixteen hours for a costume designer on any given film. It is an exhausting job, requiring vast reserves of patience and stamina. Whether it's a scene with one character or 10,000 extras, costume designers collaborate closely with their crew – the assistant costume designer, the costume illustrator, costume supervisor, set costumers, and the costume workroom. Together they create a budget and costume breakdown (determining the number of costumes needed) and manufacture, rent, purchase and fit each costume. To quote James Acheson about his SPIDER-MAN crew, "Without their skills, knowledge and stamina we could not have done it."

Never before in the history of filmmaking have costume designers worked in so many genres on so many continents. The beauty of these motion pictures reflects the dedication and talent of brilliant designers. High or low budget, from gritty urban hip-hop to sandaled Hellenic epic, costume design provides the substance and style for Hollywood guts and glamour. And designers work very hard to make it look so easy. Costume designers are often asked the innocent question, "Where did you get it?" Their answer is: we designed it. When a film captures the public's imagination, the costumes can ignite worldwide fashion trends and influence global culture. By examining the research materials, sketches and costumes of the individual designers featured in this exhibition, we hope to shine a light on the process of costume design and the vital role designers play in helping the director tell the story.

filmography note: A.A. NOMINATION – INDICATES ACADEMY AWARD® NOMINEE FOR COSTUME DESIGN
A.A. WINNER – ACADEMY AWARD® WINNER FOR COSTUME DESIGN

JAMES ACHESON

The truth is, I had never read a SPIDER-MAN comic in my life. The first time that I met Sam Raimi was on the Sony lot and he only wanted to talk about Peter Parker. By the time I got around to talking about Spider-Man it was time for Sam to leave. He said, "We can talk on the plane." We had a 5-hour meeting at 38,000 ft. when we sorted out ideas for a "new look Spidey" but the further we wandered from the famous iconic image, the less truthful it looked. It's a big enough leap of faith to believe that Peter Parker could build this suit in his bedroom in Queens. It had to look simple, it had to be extremely flexible and "look slim and athletic with a flying harness hidden underneath!" It was a sod of a frock to get right.

Firstly they had difficulty casting the actor. In desperation, I picked 25 good bodies, made them strip down and invited Sam to "pick a body type for Spider-Man." Sam picked a 6' 1" Adonis and seven weeks later chose the 5' 7" Tobey McGuire. We had already started screen testing our Adonis only to realise we had to start over. The under-suit is a 4-way stretch power net onto which is laminated a sculpted set of foam latex muscles. These stretch over the actor's torso with added sculpting subtle enough not to be noticed, yet strong enough to strengthen the power of the silhouette. This is customized for Tobey and the five stuntmen who wear the 35 suits. Made from Millaskin©, the Spidey suits' 16 pieces contain over 70 silkscreen prints of a computerized mesh print that configures to the musculature of the muscle suit, creating a trompe l'oeil effect. The shoe/boots are built by hand and glued inside the suit. Over the suit is glued a foam latex web created with the precision of a C.T.C., laser-cut aluminium mould. The gluing down of the web was done by hand and took 80 hours per suit. The problems of a 4-way stretch suit worn by 5 different people posed huge problems for the people who constructed it. Without their skills, knowledge and stamina we could not have done it.

· FILMOGRAPHY ·

TIME BANDITS (1981) · MONTY PYTHON'S THE MEANING OF LIFE (1983) · BULLSHOT (1983)
BRAZIL (1985) · WATER (1985) · HIGHLANDER (1986) · BIGGLES: ADVENTURES IN TIME (1986)
THE LAST EMPEROR (1987) [A.A. WINNER] · DANGEROUS LIAISONS [A.A. WINNER] (1988)
THE SHELTERING SKY (1990) · WUTHERING HEIGHTS (1992) · LITTLE BUDDHA (1993)
MARY SHELLEY'S FRANKENSTEIN (1994) · RESTORATION [A.A. WINNER] (1995)
THE WIND IN THE WILLOWS (1996) · THE MAN IN THE IRON MASK (1998)
THE LITTLE VAMPIRE (2000) · SPIDER-MAN (2002) · DAREDEVIL (2003) · SPIDER-MAN 2 (2004)

Red and blue four-way stretch Millaskin©
bodysuit made of 16 fabric pieces,
containing over 70 computerized
silkscreen prints. Laser cut foam latex
web is glued onto the suit.
Designed for Tobey Maguire as
Spider-Man in SPIDER-MAN (2002).

DEENA APPEL

Austin Powers is a fashion photographer and gentleman spy lost in a contemporary time, with the trappings of his own larger-than-life world. Austin's signature silhouette started with research from Carnaby Street and the mod era, but I found more reference in the world of music than the world of fashion, and particularly in George Harrison, who was quite a dandy. I looked at source material from the '60s, Pop Art, dresses made out of plastic, feathers, extreme design, couturiers Rudy Gernreich, Cardin and Couregges, magazines and films from the period, including the Bond films. We started with obscure and extremely stylized films like THE TENTH VICTIM and DANGER DIABOLIQUE.

The director and I decided early that we wanted a recognizably signature silhouette for Austin Powers. The suit fabrics would change, but the silhouette would become his most iconographic image. Much of the costume design stemmed from trying to create separate worlds for Austin and Dr. Evil, which were not scripted. Austin's world was always an explosion of color, while Dr. Evil's could be monochromatic. In the first Austin Powers film, the original suit was striped in light and royal blue. We wanted to top it in the second film and Austin ended up in a checked suit that was a cacophony of rainbow colors. By the time we came to the third film, where Austin hosts a big bash at his swinging bachelor pad – he was the centerpiece in a room full of color and I needed something that would pop. Austin's world was very textural and very plush and I felt orange velvet would be the answer. Ultimately I found beige, upholstery weight, herringbone chenille, which dyed up exquisitely into a bright burnt orange. Luckily the suit was constructed by tailor Tommy Velasco, a genius, the only one who could actually construct beautiful suits out of upholstery fabric, and line them with vintage silk.

People have asked how Mike Myers was involved in my decision-making. It's not often that a star has created a unique, one of a kind character that he's breathed life into. Mike was a great editor. He never said, "This is what I want," but rather, he had very strong feeling for a color.

10

· FILMOGRAPHY ·
HE SAID SHE SAID (1991) · 8 SECONDS (1994) · MOTHER'S BOYS (1994)
HOLY MATRIMONY (1994) · AUSTIN POWERS: INTERNATIONAL MAN OF MYSTERY (1997)
AUSTIN POWERS: THE SPY WHO SHAGGED ME (1999) · MYSTERY ALASKA (1999) · BEDAZZLED (2000)
THE TIME MACHINE (2002) · AUSTIN POWERS IN GOLDMEMBER (2002) · STUCK ON YOU (2003)

1960s-style suit of upholstery weight herringbone cotton chenille. White cotton shirt with lace trimmed sleeves and jabot. White leather belt with black boots and pink silk socks. Designed for Mike Myers as Austin Powers in AUSTIN POWERS IN GOLDMEMBER (2002).

11

COLLEEN ATWOOD

The overall design for BIG FISH was tricky because the director, Tim Burton, wanted to weave fantasy and reality, but not have a huge separation between the two. We skipped through time from modern day back to the '30s, weaving them together in the way somebody's memory might construct it. The costume for Mister Soggybottom is actually based on an old circus photograph that Tim and I have loved for years and finally found the right movie in which to use it. The character of Soggybottom is a lawyer slash circus clown, and watching the movie the audience thinks that the hero has made him up, but at the end of the film he is revealed to be a real person. Soggy appears in the 1950s, 1970s and then at the funeral; however the time periods in the film weren't designed as consecutive chronological units, but changed scene by scene. We had so much to reveal in very small cinematic moments so that the audience didn't get dizzy every time there was a new outfit and a new period.

The clown costume was built on shoulder straps with a wide hoop for the waist, and worn by a little person named Deep Roy. It had a cage built inside it, a little box that could take the weight of a dog. Actually the dog was really great and Deep Roy was really great with him, and the costume worked like a charm. The dog would stay in there and come out on cue. I took an old thin cotton chintz Halloween fabric, silkscreened it to get the over-scale circus pattern that I needed, then hand sewed sequins on the edges of the diamonds to make it even more magical. The other costumes in the scene were recreations of '50s circus troupe costumes, using actual contemporary circus performers. I met amazing people who were third and fourth generation circus people and I really learned how a circus worked. For their costumes it wasn't different than designing a dance costume or any other functional costume. In the beginning they were a little hesitant, because they really wanted to wear their own trademark ensembles; but at the end of the day they were all really happy.

· FILMOGRAPHY ·

BRING ON THE NIGHT (1985) · MANHUNTER (1986) · SOMEONE TO WATCH OVER ME (1987)

MARRIED TO THE MOB (1988) · TORCH SONG TRILOGY (1988) · THE HANDMAID'S TALE (1990)

JOE VERSUS THE VOLCANO (1990) · EDWARD SCISSORHANDS (1990) · THE SILENCE OF THE LAMBS (1991)

RUSH (1991) · LORENZO'S OIL (1992) · PHILADELPHIA (1993) · WYATT EARP (1994)

ED WOOD (1994) · LITTLE WOMEN (1994) [A.A. NOMINATION] · THE JUROR (1996)

THAT THING YOU DO (1996) · MARS ATTACKS (1996) · BUDDY (1997) · GATTACA (1997)

FALLEN (1998) · BELOVED (1998) [A.A. NOMINATION] · SLEEPY HOLLOW (1999) [A.A. NOMINATION]

THE MEXICAN (2001) · PLANET OF THE APES (2001) · CHICAGO (2002) [A.A. WINNER]

BIG FISH (2003) · LEMONY SNICKET'S A SERIES OF UNFORTUNATE EVENTS (2004)

Black and off-white cotton "vintage" silk-screened diamond print clown suit with silver sequins. Green and black three-tiered ruff, red Turkish-style shiny shoes and pointed hat. Designed for Deep Roy as Mr. Soggybottom in BIG FISH (2003).

KYM
BARRETT

I read the script of THE MATRIX in 1997 and loved it. Two years later my agent said, "Nobody wants to make it because it's too left of center." The following week, I was introduced to the Wachowski brothers at a barbeque. During my subsequent interview they asked what I thought of the script. It reminded me of a cross between a Chinese and samurai movie and a western, the only two genres I saw as a little kid living on an island in the Indian Ocean. Everybody would sit outside under their umbrellas, and on Sunday nights we had the westerns, and on Tuesday nights we had the Chinese and samurai movies. The highlight of my life was going to the movies. Andy and Larry were very emotive in their character descriptions. They wanted Trinity (Carrie-Anne Moss) to feel like "an oil slick, slippery like mercury, like she can slip through your fingers." They definitely weren't thinking about a period or fashion. The characters in MATRIX would need functional clothes for the roles they played in their own universe.

In THE MATRIX RELOADED, Neo (Keanu Reeves) had found his crusade like a knight searching for the Holy Grail. He gains stature and confidence about his abilities and a belief in himself. His costume was a Chinese robe married with a religious cassock. Because Keanu had to fly, the costume had to work aerodynamically and hide the harness while allowing his body to look good without too much fabric flapping around. We had Chinese wiremen working with us and my job was to help design the harnesses for specific flying stunts. The clerical collar made Keanu stand up straight. He is otherwise quite shy and self-effacing and tends to be very relaxed. I chose fabrics to either reflect light or help characters disappear, or create a shadow from a great silhouette when backlit. It took up so much of my brain just figuring out how to combine all these elements there wasn't time to think, "How stylish does it look?" The costumes were based on function – in their (the characters') world and in ours, which I think was its great success. People accepted it because it seemed logical in the landscape of the movie.

· FILMOGRAPHY ·
WILLIAM SHAKESPEARE'S ROMEO & JULIET (1996) · ZERO EFFECT (1998) · THE MATRIX (1999)
THREE KINGS (1999) RED PLANET (2000) · FROM HELL (2001) · THE MATRIX RELOADED (2003)
THE MATRIX REVOLUTIONS (2003) · GOTHIKA (2003)

Floor-length black wool cassock with
mandarin collar. Black cotton dress shirt
and wool trousers. Black leather lace-up
ankle boots with square wooden heel.
Designed for Keanu Reeves as Neo
in THE MATRIX RELOADED (2003).

JENNY BEAVAN

POSSESSION was set in 2000 and, in a non-specific way, the 1860s – but the director, Neil LaBute, was looking for a heightened reality rather than an accurate reproduction of the period. The film fell into two distinct sections: the modern story, particularly Gwyneth Paltrow's clothes, had an icy feel, whereas the Victorian story was more appropriate in dusty pinks and olive greens with turquoise blue.

With only seven weeks prep time, I had to work very fast. Normally it takes time to find my way to a character, but in this case I took my initial clues from looking at the pre-Raphaelite painters. I like the process to be gradual – the thinking time between fittings when one's mind drifts around ideas is an important part of the creative process. Often, the solution appears as a blinding flash when doing something mundane like household shopping in a supermarket.

I don't usually think of a specific piece of clothing before I start pulling together items that might be useful. I feel that my collaboration with the actor is what makes the costume work. The costumes really evolve during the fitting, with the actor's body language and a pooling of ideas, and it's at that point that specific items can become important. I normally fit the actor at the first meeting, we have a "dress up" session to look at shapes and colours and initial concepts. Sometimes the actor is cast so late that I only get one chance to do this – and it concerns me that some film companies lack understanding of the time it takes to do a good fitting and make a good costume.

I also create a scrapbook or "mood board," to give the director and actors a sense of the costumes. Each character in POSSESSION was defined by color but the effect was natural, although it was actually fairly tightly controlled. My costumes are always "story driven": for example, the character Christabel, although Victorian, was strong – a feminist, and a practical woman – which was reflected in her clothes, such as skirts that hitched up for the beach at whim.

The budget did not allow for everything to be made new, so the modern women's clothes were purchased. Fashion houses contributed some clothes for Gwyneth's modern character; it was my challenge to mix them up and make the labels "disappear." The Victorian men's clothing was from stock and re-fitted, dyed, and customized. The final costumes were a real mixture of old and new, created from scratch or customized from existing clothes, to fit the demands of the character and story.

· FILMOGRAPHY ·

JANE AUSTIN IN MANHATTAN (1980) · THE BOSTONIANS (1984) [A.A. NOMINATION WITH JOHN BRIGHT]
A ROOM WITH A VIEW (1986) [A.A. WINNER WITH JOHN BRIGHT]
MAURICE (1987) [A.A. NOMINATION WITH JOHN BRIGHT] · A SUMMER STORY (1988)
THE DECEIVERS (1988) · MOUNTAINS OF THE MOON (1990) · IMPROMPTU (1991) · WHITE FANG (1991)
THE BRIDGE (1992) · HOWARD'S END (1992) [A.A. NOMINATION WITH JOHN BRIGHT]
SWING KIDS (1993) · REMAINS OF THE DAY (1993) [A.A. NOMINATION WITH JOHN BRIGHT]
BLACK BEAUTY (1994) · JEFFERSON IN PARIS (1995) · JANE EYRE (1996)
SENSE AND SENSIBILITY (1995) [A.A. NOMINATION WITH JOHN BRIGHT] · METROLAND (1997)
EVER AFTER (1998) · TEA WITH MUSSOLINI (1999) · ANNA AND THE KING (1999) [A.A. NOMINATION]
GOSFORD PARK (2001) [A.A. NOMINATION] · POSSESSION (2002) · TIMELINE (2003)
ALEXANDER (2004) · CASANOVA (2004)

CHRISTABEL — First meeting with Ash
'Crabb-Robinson' dinner.
Kingfisher blue velvet dress with smocked cuffs
Antique glass buttons, sash and girdle.
John Bright   POSSESSION 2000

1890s-style kingfisher blue evening robe of silk velvet with plaited velvet girdle and gold braid. Undergarments include corset and crinoline. Designed for Jennifer Ehle as Cristabel LaMotte in POSSESSION (2002).

MARK BRIDGES

What's great about a director who writes his own material is that designers get answers. There is a complete vision, and an ability to evolve with other collaborators and not lose that vision. Paul Thomas Anderson, the writer/director of PUNCH-DRUNK LOVE, had lived and worked the script for many months and was very open to anything you wanted to bring to the table for the visuals of the film. Initially for inspiration, Paul suggested the production team watch a variety of films such as the Rogers/Astaire musical CAREFREE, AN AMERICAN IN PARIS, THE BANDWAGON and A WOMAN IS A WOMAN, to name a few. Paul had always known that he wanted Adam Sandler's character Barry in a suit, and we were taken by the vibrant blues in the Technicolor films of the early 1950s. With these inspirations, I gathered a series of blue fabric swatches ranging from very saturated to very bright blue. Paul walked into my office, gravitated to that bright blue piece of fabric and said, "Should we go this far?" And something clicked for him.

What is also interesting about PUNCH-DRUNK LOVE is that the production design provided white and neutral backgrounds for the costumes to play against. Also, Paul writes films that make a lot of verbal references to a character's clothes and personal style. The first time we see Barry he is alone at work and when his co-workers arrive they notice – "Hey, you bought a new suit!" He replies, "Yeah, I thought I'd like to dress up." From the start we establish Barry as uncomfortable in his own skin. Adam Sandler was very open and accepting to anything we wanted to do with the costumes. As long as he was physically comfortable he was good with any color. During the design process we tried other costume variations but ultimately it came down to Paul's decision to keep Barry in the blue suit for the entire film.

Reviewing my fitting photos of the process, it's actually a combination of two different suits to get the final silhouette; the pants were inspired by a Jil Sander shape and the jacket shape by Zegna. Only the changing of Barry's neckties indicates any kind of emotional or script day change. We used the blue suit to visually tell a story, although there is not any character arc like moving from rags to riches. There are beautiful shots in the film of the way the suit moves and changes color in different lighting situations. Barry's costume also make a visual connection with those of his love interest, Lena. PUNCH-DRUNK LOVE was the ideal collaboration between costume design, camera, production design, acting and directing.

18

· FILMOGRAPHY ·

HARD EIGHT (1996) · BOOGIE NIGHTS (1997) · CAN'T HARDLY WAIT (1998)) · BLAST FROM THE PAST (1999)
DEEP BLUE SEA (1999) · MAGNOLIA (1999) · BLOW (2001) · PUNCH-DRUNK LOVE (2002) · 8 MILE (2002)
THE ITALIAN JOB (2003) · I HEART HUCKABEE'S (2004) · BE COOL (2004)

Two-piece bright blue wool gabardine
suit with white button-front shirt.
Designed for Adam Sandler as Barry Egan
in PUNCH-DRUNK LOVE (2002).

19

KRISTIN BURKE

Before I went in to interview for THE COOLER I was told to come totally prepared with a completely realized design. I came up with a concept of character: Bernie Lootz's clothes going from bigger to smaller (sloppy to fitted), and from cool colors to warm colors (disconnected to connected). The interview went really well, and they called me back for a second one. There were three producers, the director, the production designer and then an actor who came in to have an audition. About ten minutes into the interview they all started talking, and didn't say another word to me. I was sitting in the room with these costume sketches thinking, "Did they like it?" I left the interview and I called my agent and I said, "I think I blew it. They just started talking, I don't know what happened..." and he said, "Kristin, I think they just had their first design meeting!"

Director Wayne Kramer and I didn't really have discussions once we went into production because he had bought my design concept (fit and color) from the beginning. Wayne was looking for something that would really push William Macy's character of Bernie Lootz into a hyper reality. I explained that the audience would not consciously perceive Bernie's costume changes, but they will be affected by them. The film begins with washed out, fluorescent cool colors of blue and green that Bernie wears when he is a poor, sad loser. We realize that Bernie has bloomed when the costume colors turn vibrant and he feels love; the lighting is warm – he's a changed man. Bernie's color palette is specific to his character. We have a lot of greens in the movie – green representing luck and money. From a graphic standpoint, straight lines and curvy lines make people feel differently, and shape has very subtle influences on the human psyche. When we have curvy lines, droopy, curvy, sagging lines, we tend to feel pity for that person. Bernie's initially unkempt, he doesn't take care of himself, and by the end of the film his lines are crisp and tailored. Bernie's costume changes are motivated by his state of mind and his emotional arc.

· FILMOGRAPHY ·

STAR MAPS (1997) · THE CORPORATE LADDER (1997) · RAVAGER (1997) · TACTICAL ASSAULT (1998)
SHARK IN A BOTTLE (1998) · THE MATING HABITS OF THE EARTHBOUND HUMAN (1999)
TERROR TRACT (2000) · THE BRANIACS.COM (2000) · RACE TO SPACE (2001)
THE COOLER (2003) · BRING IT ON AGAIN (2004)

Taupe poly/wool blend suit and green cotton shirt. Handmade yellow vintage silk tie. Fishbone weave leather belt and distressed kiltie loafers, both in oxblood. Designed for William H. Macy as Bernie Lootz in THE COOLER (2003).

MILENA CANONERO

This gown was one of the 18th century costumes that I designed for AFFAIR OF THE NECKLACE, with Joely Richardson playing the doomed Marie Antoinette. The time period was a few years before the French revolution. Joely was much taller than the real Marie Antoinette and the dress needed to create a silhouette of natural elegance. I had a beautiful genuine18th century piece embroidered with four peacocks. We cut the peacocks out, divided them and appliquéd two of them to the bodice of the dress and two of them down across the skirt. It gave an interesting look, instead of just an otherwise ordinary classical 1780s dress. The original embroidery was on a gorgeous piece of fabric, which I matched for the dress. The imagery of peacocks was appealing because they are a traditional symbol of bad luck, and I liked the idea of using them for Marie Antoinette. In this extended sequence she's descending the staircase of the grand opera house, surrounded by all of her ladies-in-waiting.

I have collected antique laces for a long time, and I used pieces from my collection for this film. The trim on this gown was 18th century original lace pulled from my storage. I used it around the décolleté neckline and it gave a nice rich look to the costume – as the silhouette of the gown was kept very simple. I finished it off with a very pretty birdcage head ornament with a canary inside, a real canary. For the long shots I had a fake canary, but for the close ups we placed a live canary in the cage that was attached to Joely's wig. If you look at some original gowns from that period they can be pretty heavy and boring, but we gave it a slightly pristine angle. With the peacock embroidery and the birdcage canary, it looked very, very fashionable. The authentic period jewelry was all rented. On her feet she wore white satin 18th century shoes made by Pompeii in Rome with beautiful antique buckles, and she carried a lovely 18th century fan. It was really a charming, complete outfit for that kind of appearance at a formal public event in Paris for an aristocratic lady.

· FILMOGRAPHY ·

A CLOCKWORK ORANGE (1971) · BARRY LYNDON (1975) [A.A. WINNER WITH ULLA-BRITT SODERLUND]
MIDNIGHT EXPRESS (1978) · THE SHINING (1980) · CHARIOTS OF FIRE (1981) [A.A. WINNER] · THE HUNGER (1983)
GIVE MY REGARDS TO BROAD STREET (1984) · THE COTTON CLUB (1984) · OUT OF AFRICA (1985) [A.A. NOMINATION]
BARFLY (1987) · TUCKER: THE MAN AND HIS DREAM (1988) [A.A. NOMINATION] · DICK TRACY (1990) [A.A. NOMINATION]
THE GODFATHER: PART III (1990) · THE BACHELOR (1991) · SINGLE WHITE FEMALE (1992) · FATALE (1992)
ONLY YOU (1994) · LOVE AFFAIR (1994) · CAMILLA (1994) · DEATH AND THE MAIDEN (1994) · BULWORTH (1998)
TANGO (1998) · TITUS (1999) [A.A. NOMINATION] · THE AFFAIR OF THE NECKLACE (2001) [A.A. NOMINATION]
SOLARIS (2002) · THE LIFE AQUATIC (2004) · OCEAN'S TWELVE (2004)

1780s aristocratic court dress of pale ivory
duchesse 18th-century silk satin with original
peacock silk appliqué embroidery and
original 18th-century lace trim.
Designed for Joely Richardson as Marie-Antoinette in
THE AFFAIR OF THE NECKLACE (2001).

23

SOPHIE DE RAKOFF CARBONELL

The costumes from LEGALLY BLONDE 2 are more stylized than in the first movie, and Charlie Herman-Wurmfeld, the director on the second movie, was very trusting. We had the same production designer and actors, and Mark Platt was the producer of both films. It was Reese Witherspoon, the production designer and myself working together on the look of each movie and we were very much left to our own devices both times. LEGALLY BLONDE 2 turned the stereotype of the dumb blonde on its head with Elle Woods having an internship at one of the most powerful law offices in Washington. That's where we meet her at the beginning of the second movie. A little later on we find Elle walking up the steps to Congress. How did we want to see her walking through the doors of Congress? Who was the most stylish iconic woman to have come out of the White House? It had to be Jackie Kennedy. That pink suit was the first costume I thought of, and from the very beginning every other costume moved on either side of it.

When we were building the costume we looked at all different shades of pink and all different fabrics. Pink was always the Elle Woods signature color but we actually did less pink in the sequel. The company that built the suit had a vintage silk wool linen fabric from the '60s already existing in the perfect color.

The great thing about the camera tests was that I've seen the costume many times - because I've had multiple fittings with Reese. Then, I looked at that pink pillbox hat and thought, "Oh my God, it's so costumey, I've gone too far!" But the minute Reese got in front of the camera and came up on the video monitor the whole costume came alive, it was amazing. It's completely over the top but it's just perfect. Reese can get away with a lot of stuff, especially as Elle Woods – who's a girlie girl character but underneath it all is an instinctive feminist. That's why it's always endlessly fun to create costumes for Elle Woods.

· FILMOGRAPHY ·

SATURN (1999) · CRIME AND PUNISHMENT IN SUBURBIA (2000) · FOUR DOGS PLAYING POKER (2000)
THE CENTER OF THE WORLD (2001) · LEGALLY BLONDE (2001) · ALL ABOUT THE BENJAMINS (2002)
SWEET HOME ALABAMA (2002) · DALLAS 362 (2003) · LEGALLY BLONDE 2: RED, WHITE & BLONDE (2003)
GRAND THEFT PARSONS (2003) · SHALL WE DANCE? (2004) · IN HER SHOES (2004)

Single-breasted notch lapel long black suede coat
with black knit turtleneck and black trousers.
Designed for Samuel L. Jackson
as John Shaft in SHAFT (2000).

27

SHAY CUNLIFFE

In WHAT A GIRL WANTS, Daphne, a New York teenager, sets off for England with a backpack to discover her long lost father – who turns out to be Colin Firth, a Lord. To make the story work, we decided to try it in a world that was contemporary but belonged to the land of fiction. Costuming was the only way that we could lead the story in that direction. To allow our heroine Daphne, Amanda Bynes, to be a streetwise kid who wears faded bellbottoms and chunky platforms, we had to keep the English girls dressed in a much more conventional way, so that they play against each other. We needed to make our statement very strongly.

For her first debutante ball Daphne's stepmother and sister set her up for miserable failure. "We'll find something for you," and they leave a disgustingly hideous dress on her bed that no teenager could put on. This film is a comedy, so when Daphne is revealed standing in the dress, you laugh. It's beyond anything anyone could really buy in a shop. We see Daphne looking at herself in despair... and grabbing a pair of scissors. Later at the ball, when she begins down the grand staircase, she has turned it into a one-shouldered gown, cut away all of the ugly chiffon over-layers to the lining fabric, and it's passably elegant.

This gown had to originate out of the first hideous dress, and I wish that we had been able to show more of her cutting into it. We made the second dress with the fiction that it is the lining of the first one, embellished by its extra fabric. The original gown is three horrible layers of circular chiffon that fall in a neo-sixties droopy way. The party is a terrible flop but then Daphne gets everyone up dancing, so the dress not only had to be sexy and hot, but it really had to move. I conceived of a gown full of dance elements – all of the pieces fly out as she started twirling and all of the bits of chiffon she draped around the shoulders start moving too. It was really a dress conceived for motion.

· FILMOGRAPHY ·

MRS. SOFFEL (1984) · D.A.R.Y.L. (1985) · THE MANHATTAN PROJECT (1986) · THE BELIEVERS (1987)
MIRACLE MILE (1988) · MILES FROM HOME (1988) · WAIT UNTIL SPRING · BANDINI (1989)
THE LONG WALK HOME (1990) · FIRES WITHIN (1991) · OF MICE AND MEN (1992)
BOUND BY HONOR (1993) · THE MAN WITHOUT A FACE (1993) · DOLORES CLAIBORNE (1995)
LONE STAR (1996) · MULTIPLICITY (1996) · TRIAL AND ERROR (1997) · CITY OF ANGELS (1998)
A CIVIL ACTION (1998) · LIMBO (1999) · THE STORY OF US (1999) · THE PRIME GIG (2000)
SWEET NOVEMBER (2001) · ENOUGH (2002) · WHAT A GIRL WANTS (2003)
ALEX AND EMMA (2003) · SPARTAN (2004) · SILVER CITY (2004)

Three-tiered gown of bronze and blue iridescent silk chiffon over French blue sleeveless satin. Designed for Amanda Bynes as Daphne Reynolds in WHAT A GIRL WANTS (2003).

SUSIE DE SANTO

When Michelle Pfeiffer's character, Claire, sees Madison the ghost – played by Amber Valetta – in WHAT LIES BENEATH, she thinks she's going crazy. Director Robert Zemeckis wanted to imply that she was seeing things. The first time that Michelle sees Amber it's in the reflection of fogged mirrors. My source material for ghost imagery was art and photography, and my inspiration came from the work of watercolorist Ross Bleckner and photographers Claire Yaff, Howard Schatz, Bill Jacobson and Arno Rafael Minkkinen, who have all been fascinated with water and reflection. I did my boards for the ghost character in three parts: Amber alive, Amber as an underwater image, and Amber's reflection in water showing the movement of her clothes in water. I conceptualized taking the physical image of a person and then obscuring it, so it almost appeared as a reflection. Bob liked the idea so much that the rest of the crew worked toward that vision.

Amber wore a white dress when she was murdered. We took that dress and knit into it something that we later completely pulled apart by hand. Because the costume was worn almost exclusively underwater in the film, we wanted it to look like fishnet. As the underwater costume deteriorated and the corpse got gorier, we hand painted the costume to look more distressed and disintegrated in many different stages. Make-up man Stan Winston created the corpse puppet of Amber as she became more and more horrifying. By the end of the movie she was a skeleton with this fishnet flowing around her. We worked with Rob Legato, visual effects supervisor, to determine the placement of the ghost in the bathtub or in the mirror.

I used loose lace for the original ballerina-length dress with a deep scoop neck, and a fitted drop waist A-line gored skirt. The transparent lace had a layer of chiffon underneath which allowed for a certain grace at the end of the movie when she turns and starts to float up toward the surface. There's a photography book of underwater ballet dancers with their costumes floating around them. It's beautiful imagery of costumes in water, and this idea is translated into the film.

· FILMOGRAPHY ·

JOYSTICKS (1983) · GOLDY 2: THE SAGA OF THE GOLDEN BEAR (1986) · JOHNNY BE GOOD (1988)
JACK'S BACK (1988) · BOOK OF LOVE (1990) · EYES OF AN ANGEL (1991) · IRON MAZE (1991)
RUBY (1992) · A DANGEROUS WOMAN (1993) · TWENTY BUCKS (1993) · BAD GIRLS (1994)
STUART SAVES HIS FAMILY (1995) · THE BABY-SITTERS CLUB (1995) · ONE FINE DAY (1996)
HOPE FLOATS (1998) · THE DEEP END OF THE OCEAN (1999) · TEACHING MRS. TINGLE (1999)
WHAT LIES BENEATH (2000) · MISS CONGENIALITY (2000) · I AM SAM (2001) · THE NEW GUY (2002)
WHITE OLEANDER (2002) · LITTLE BLACK BOOK (2004) · CHRISTMAS WITH THE KRANKS (2004)

Long-sleeve pullover dress in sheer white cotton knit with hand painted distressing. Attached hand crocheted pieces tied to costume. Designed for Amber Valletta as Madison Elizabeth Frank in WHAT LIES BENEATH (2000).

31

NGILA DICKSON

Director Ed Zwick had a very strong vision for THE LAST SAMURAI; he had been developing this project for a long time and had great depth of knowledge about Japan during this time period (1873-1876). Ed wanted production designer Lilly Kilvert and me to be as accurate as possible with the sets and the costumes. We were in perfect accord in wishing to make this as true to its century, and the Japanese culture and ethic, as possible. There weren't difficulties finding the period research except for the distance to retrieve it from Japan. It took several trips between Japan and the U.S. – but this film was one of those dream projects where all the right information seemed to come to hand quite quickly. I gave myself six weeks to assemble the research and make a decision about whether we could design and manufacture the complex samurai armor ourselves (which we did). Later, in preparation for the design of the film, I divided the civilian costumes into different color palettes – sepia tones for the American scenes, indigo blue and rich dark colors and patterns for the Japanese villagers and samurai warriors. Each character could be very much identified by the color of his costume. There was enormous synchronicity between John Toll's cinematography for the film, the colors of the costumes, and the sets.

The American and Japanese armies and the samurai armor were self-defining, although I aged the colors considerably from how bright they were historically meant to be – otherwise, each detail of the uniforms was historically correct. As I was reading the script I was inspired to doodle a sketch of Tom Cruise's character, Nathan Algren; I wanted Algren's leather coat to represent the idealized American west he left behind, and most importantly, to provide his character with a sense of security. It was an old and familiar garment. Wearing that leather coat in Japan helped Algren to remain confident in a world out of control and full of political intrigue. I designed and created every costume for the principal actors in the film. A costume designer must always be flexible according to the changes that can happen during shooting – however, very little changed during the filming of THE LAST SAMURAI.

· FILMOGRAPHY ·

Ruby and Rata (1990) · User Friendly (1990) · My Grandfather Is a Vampire (1991)
Crush (1992) · The Rainbow Warrior (1992) · Jack Be Nimble (1993)
Heavenly Creatures (1994) · Peach (1995) · Young Hercules (1998)
The Lord of the Rings: The Fellowship of the Ring (2001) [A.A. nomination with Richard Taylor]
The Lord of the Rings: The Two Towers (2002) · The Last Samurai (2003) [A.A. nomination]
The Lord of the Rings: The Return of the King (2003) [A.A. winner with Richard Taylor]
Without a Paddle (2004)

Silk and leather 1860s-style red and black
Samurai armor with chain-mail, black braided
cording and gold and brass ornamentation.
Designed for Tom Cruise as Nathan Algren in
THE LAST SAMURAI (2003).

SARAH EDWARDS

"Can you start Monday?" and it was high gear all the way through the production of UPTOWN GIRLS. I did get Brittany Murphy a couple of weeks before we started shooting. Both of us saw this film as a fairy tale so the palette had more color than I usually work with, and it was a summer film so it was almost kaleidoscopic. Brittany's character, Molly Gunn, was supposed to be a whimsical young woman interested in art and fashion, and maybe she would have found clothes in her mother's closet from the '70s or the '80s. I did look at research, and we did look for vintage pieces similar to this period jumper that we have for this exhibition, a denim overall jumper from the '70s with different colored patches and embroidered flowers with Bedazzler rhinestones all over it.

My sister and I had a babysitter in the '70s who had made this jumper for my sister Kate when she was ten years old. Brittany is tiny (a size 0), and I thought, "You know that thing might fit her!" So... I had Kate dig it out of her closet and it worked really well. We even left the "Kate" embroidered on the back. Brittany was funny; she said, "Oh! Let's not cover that up. Maybe her mother's name was Kate."

I don't know if all of them ended up in the movie, but I designed thirty-nine changes for Brittany in UPTOWN GIRLS. We had to make costumes out of clothes that existed. We re-cut things and made them into almost different clothes. Some of them came from vintage dealers in New York, we bought everything, and made bits and pieces when we needed to. It was fun to do something that for me was very different. Boaz Yakin, the director, liked my ideas and with our very short prep time and a very low budget it was all very young and kind of hip and colorful.

In some ways it was challenging because I wanted everything to be neutral, classic and streamlined. But it wasn't that movie, and that's not what was required. We started talking about the character, and the mother's closet, and I started thinking about this denim jumper that I remembered, and it just was amazing that Kate still had it.

· FILMOGRAPHY ·
THE LAST DAYS OF DISCO (1998) · JACK FROST (1998) · THE PERFECT YOU (2002)
IGBY GOES DOWN (2002) · UPTOWN GIRLS (2003) · THE INTERPRETER (2004)

1970s-style denim jumper dress with applied decorations including veri-colored patchwork, embroidered flowers and applied rhinestones. Designed for Brittany Murphy as Molly Gunn in UPTOWN GIRLS (2003).

APRIL FERRY

Director Jonathan Mostow takes a while to make up his mind, but once he does, he just lets me do it. Everyone insisted on keeping the look of THE TERMINATOR, so my key design elements started with a black leather jacket, great sunglasses and Arnold's handsome face. I had an icon and a costume that was "set in stone." The Terminator's costume for the sequel had to be updated with a new and reinvented version of the previous one, but because it was so familiar there was no way for me to change the "motorcycle/biker" look. My vision of the story was different from the director's because I wanted the woman Terminator to be much sexier. Otherwise, we agreed on the overall style of the movie. With the intense action sequences, Mostow was very concerned about the actress and the stunt doubles being able to work safely and comfortably in the costume, so it was necessary to cover Kristanna Loken's body more than I wanted. I had hoped for a much barer look.

The color palette for the movie focused on hard, tough colors: red and black. My inspiration and process for the design of the costumes included color, texture/surface, silhouette, and especially emotional cues. I do think the black of the Terminator and the red of the Terminatrix were definitely character defining, since there was no particular character arc – both main characters remained the same through out the film. The Terminator did get dirtier and his costume more distressed, but the Terminatrix didn't, which was a choice of the director. Mostow's wanted to make the Terminator more vulnerable, human and sympathetic.

The costume research began when the project was still in the thinking and development stage. It took me at least six weeks to assemble my materials, and the research never ended. We created and manufactured the entire principal wardrobe, although we rented police uniforms. There was more than one second unit shooting simultaneously on the film, and each unit needed a complete set of wardrobe for doubles and stunt people. Arnold had fifty complete and identical costumes in different stages of aging, and Kristanna had thirty-five identical costumes!

· FILMOGRAPHY ·

MASK (1985) · GOTCHA! (1985) · BIG TROUBLE IN LITTLE CHINA (1986) · PLANES, TRAINS AND AUTOMOBILES (1987)
MADE IN HEAVEN (1987) · SHE'S HAVING A BABY (1988) · CHILD'S PLAY (1988) · THREE FUGITIVES (1989)
LEVIATHAN (1989) · IMMEDIATE FAMILY (1989) · ALMOST AN ANGEL (1990) · RADIO FLYER (1992)
THE BABE (1992) · UNLAWFUL ENTRY (1992) · FREE WILLY (1993) · BEETHOVEN'S 2ND (1993)
MAVERICK (1994) [A.A. NOMINATION] · LITTLE GIANTS (1994) · THE ASSOCIATE (1996) · SHADOW CONSPIRACY (1997)
LITTLE BOY BLUE (1997) · FLUBBER (1997) · CLAUDINE'S RETURN (1998) · PLAYING BY HEART (1998)
BROKEDOWN PALACE (1999) · U-571 (2000) · BOYS AND GIRLS (2000) · DONNIE DARKO (2001) · 15 MINUTES (2001)
FRAILTY (2001) · NATIONAL SECURITY (2003) · TERMINATOR 3: RISE OF THE MACHINES (2003)

Black leather jacket and trousers with fitted
black tee-shirt with mock-turtleneck.
Designed for Arnold Schwarzenegger as Terminator in
TERMINATOR 3: RISE OF THE MACHINES (2003).

BRUCE FINLAYSON

I collaborated with director Bill Condon on GODS AND MONSTERS for five years from inception to shoot. A lot of time was spent getting it right. I'm pretty thorough about my research. We all try to put our best work into everything we do, whether it's huge, or a three million dollar film. One doesn't scrimp because it's a lower budget. We only had two big set pieces, including one for a 1955 garden party at George Cukor's house, when Princess Margaret was in attendance. There's only one costume – I based it on what I remembered of the time and what I could find in London. We didn't have any references for that George Cukor party; in fact, Bill and I and Richard Sherman, the production designer, didn't want to be absolutely specific about period. We wanted to have a little bit of freeness, but obviously Margaret was as big with her feathered hats as was her mother.

I worked on a low scale palette apart from Ian McKellen's costumes. Red was his color, and we gave him red vests and red ties and red stripes. Margaret was black and white. Richard had black and white with canopies everywhere and black and white candles. For Margaret I borrowed pearls, a pearl and faux diamond bracelet, and a pair of diamond earrings from my mother. I had a lot of pictorial reference to show to the actress – she got the general feeling of Margaret's tendency to overdress. The dress has its own stiffened petticoat, and it's silk faille ivory with a black polka dot, strapless with a little bolero jacket. She wore a garter belt and proper hose and long kid gloves above her elbows. The dress has a black silk velvet bow hanging right down to the hem at the front, and it's princess line, of course. I talk to designers and I hear some horror stories, and I realize how blessed I am to have met Bill and worked with him, because it really does make one's life a hell of a lot easier.

Strapless Princess line with Bolero jacket. Jacket has short sleeves and 1" stand at nape of neck.

Ivory silk faille with black polka dot. Black velvet tie. Hat of self fabric ostrich plumes.

Mid-1950s ivory and black polka dot silk faille strapless dress with black silk velvet bow and matching short sleeve bolero jacket. Designed for Cornelia Hayes O'Herlihy as Princess Margaret in GODS AND MONSTERS (1998).

39

MARIE FRANCE

For Martin Lawrence's character Jamal Walker (aka Skywalker) in BLACK KNIGHT I created a medieval version of a hip-hop outfit, in suede and leather. I took the research for this comedy as seriously as if I was doing a dramatic piece. I talked to armorers, studied illustrations and paintings and then decided on a specific era of the Middle Ages.

At the outset, Martin Lawrence is working in a failing theme park when he falls from a bridge into a castle moat while trying to retrieve a medallion. When he comes to, he is in the Middle Ages. As in present day he is wearing a very bright green football jersey and baggy jeans, he really stands out.

Eventually Jamal endears himself to the king and becomes an important character at the royal court. In this new incarnation, he orders clothes to reflect his elevated position. He wants contemporary pop clothes but they would have to be manufactured using only materials which would have been available to the people of the Middle Ages. Everything about his new outfit was consistent to the making of clothing in those days including the more muted colors, but with a hip-hop style. I thought it would be funny for Martin Lawrence to still be the only one totally out of sync at the court. The V-neck football jersey is now in green leather with some details in suede, like a logo patch in front and stripes around the neck and the sleeves; his pants are a new version of his oversized jeans but made in light brown suede with overstitching in leather.

The director, Gil Junger, originally wanted to make the movie dark and dirty, a harsh world close to that of BRAVEHEART. So, we started shooting the peasant rebellion very gritty and realistic. Later the studio had a different idea and wanted more of a fairytale vision. By the time we came to the castle I had made the costumes brighter and the film became more of a fantasy. In the end it works, because the change in palette represented the two different worlds of the period. Life in the royal court was more opulent and colorful, which contrasted with the grim reality of the rebels in the woods.

· FILMOGRAPHY ·

PURPLE RAIN (1984) · UNDER THE CHERRY MOON (1986) · BILL & TED'S BOGUS JOURNEY (1991)
STOP! OR MY MOM WILL SHOOT (1992) · ENCINO MAN (1992) · BUFFY THE VAMPIRE SLAYER (1992)
CONEHEADS (1993) · TOM AND HUCK (1995) · GRIDLOCK'D (1997) · KEYS TO TULSA (1997)
THE BORROWERS (1997) · THE WONDERFUL ICE CREAM SUIT (1998) · BLACK KNIGHT (2001)
THE DANGEROUS LIVES OF ALTAR BOYS (2002) · NEVER DIE ALONE (2004) · GARFIELD: THE MOVIE (2004)

Medieval-style hip-hop costume. Pullover sports-style jersey in forest green leather with overstitched and painted suede patches. Carmel suede trousers. Designed for Martin Lawrence as Jamal Walker (aka Skywalker) in BLACK KNIGHT (2001).

41

GLORIA GRESHAM

BANDITS is a road movie. The guys break out of prison in Oregon and work their way down the coast of California until they get to Los Angeles, and that is exactly how it was shot. The key elements of the costumes support the characters; they needed to be contemporary and character friendly. Since most films are shot from the waist up, I find color and texture to become more important than the silhouette. Of course, the principal actors, Cate Blanchett, Billy Bob Thornton and Bruce Willis, bring their personalities and talents to the visualization. Billy Bob's character is a germ freak, so we kept him more or less sterile looking with lots of white, but with a flare. Bruce's character was more of a dandy, including handsome leather jackets and well cut clothes and Cate's character was a repressed housewife gone wild. She is a great actress and really understands the process of costume development. There were very few changes in the costumes after the initial fittings. I believe this is because of my long-time collaboration with director Barry Levinson, and a brilliant cast.

I have been the costume designer on ten Barry Levinson films, and he communicates his thoughts very well. Even though the film takes place in the present, he does like a touch of retro or stylized design from time to time. It took me about a month to put together the research portfolio. I do research on every project, be it contemporary or period; it requires this design process. The opening scene of the film is a state prison, which always has specific needs. For BANDITS, I used the usual books, magazines, catalogs and especially photos of real bank robbers.

Every day of shooting there was coordination with the Hair and Makeup Department. All of the principal actors had headwear and disguises that were important story points. Billy Bob wore several wigs as part of his disguise for robbing banks. Bruce mostly relied on hats and Cate loved the hats, headscarves and wig changes. The costume designer's work should always enhance the audience's understanding of the characters and situations in that film.

· FILMOGRAPHY ·

Just Tell Me What You Want (1980) · Urban Cowboy (1980) · Zorro, The Gay Blade (1981)
Diner (1982) · The Escape Artist (1982) · Author! Author! (1982)
Without a Trace (1983) · Footloose (1984) · The Natural (1984) · Body Double (1984)
Fletch (1985) · 8 Million Ways to Die (1986) · Outrageous Fortune (1987) · Tin Men (1987)
Midnight Run (1988) · Twins (1998) · Ghostbusters II (1989) · When Harry Met Sally (1989)
The War of the Roses (1989) · Avalon (1990) [a.a. nomination] · Misery (1990)
Kindergarten Cop (1990) · V. I. Warshawski (1991) · Beethoven (1992) · A Few Good Men (1992)
Last Action Hero (1993) · North (1994) · Disclosure (1994) · Boys on the Side (1995)
The American President (1995) · Sleepers (1996) · Ghosts of Mississippi (1996) · Sphere (1998)
Six Days Seven Nights (1998) · Liberty Heights (1999) · Rules of Engagement (2000) · The Kid (2000)
Bandits (2001) · The Hunted (2003) · Envy (2004) · The Last Shot (2004)

Off-white cashmere sport jacket with gray flannel
trousers, custom made white cotton shirt and silk tie.
Raglan sleeved taupe micro-fiber belted trench coat.
Designed for Billy Bob Thornton as
Terry Lee Collins in BANDITS (2001).

BETSY HEIMANN

The research for ALMOST FAMOUS was compiled from photographs from a 1973 Neil Young tour as well as other tours that Cameron Crowe had been on. We looked at these photos together and decided to make a love letter to that period of music when the romance was still in rock, and rock as a business was beginning to rise. I wanted to combine Kate Hudson's personality with Penny Lane, a legendary 'band aide.' Her character reminded me of the Jimi Hendrix song "Little Wing." Some of the lyrics are: "When I'm sad she comes to me with a thousand smiles, she gives to me for free. It's all right, she says, it's all right. Take anything you want from me, anything." It suggests a person who never stops giving even if doesn't always feel good. To me, that was Penny Lane.

Cameron had said once that he wanted Penny to evoke the spirit of Shirley Maclaine's character in THE APARTMENT. That was the direction for the Penny Lane coat, and that's what he always called it before I even designed it. We wanted her to appear in the beginning, standing on the top of the ramp as a goddess of the 'band aides;' a radiant young girl in a coat that wrapped all her emotions in a beautiful exterior that she could hide within.

Even though all of Penny Lane's clothes were custom made, it was important to me that they looked authentic. All the fabrics were overdyed to look older and we controlled the palette using colors of the period like the avocado green color of Penny's coat. I decided to give the coat a big, furry cream collar because it was very glamorous, and the cream color bounced light off Kate's face. Cinematographer John Toll and I tested different shades of cream, figuring out which would be the best for Kate's complexion. I wanted the coat to be iconic – like Marlene Dietrich, but in a '70s rock way. Her pants were made of velvet so the light reflected the curves of her body when she danced by the side of the stage. The camisole was reminiscent of a Victorian camisole as vintage shopping was coming into fashion at that time.

I knew we were successful when people saw ALMOST FAMOUS and thought that they were looking at a movie that was shopped in thrift stores.

· FILMOGRAPHY ·

SKATETOWN, U.S.A. (1979) · HIGH ROAD TO CHINA (1983) · SKY BANDITS (1986) ·
SURRENDER (1987) · ELVIRA, MISTRESS OF THE DARK (1988) · TUNE IN TOMORROW (1990)
WELCOME HOME, ROXY CARMICHAEL (1990) · ONE GOOD COP (1991) · RESERVOIR DOGS (1992)
THE ADVENTURES OF HUCK FINN (1993) · GUNMEN (1994) · RENAISSANCE MAN (1994)
PULP FICTION (1994) · THE TIE THAT BINDS (1995) · GET SHORTY (1995) · 2 DAYS IN THE VALLEY (1996)
JERRY MAGUIRE (1996) · SWITCHBACK (1997) · MERCURY RISING (1998) · OUT OF SIGHT (1998)
SIMON BIRCH (1998) · ANYWHERE BUT HERE (1999) · ALMOST FAMOUS (2000) · THE FAMILY MAN (2000)
VANILLA SKY (2001) · STEALING HARVARD (2002) · RED DRAGON (2002) · CHEER UP (2004)

1970s avocado and cream wool coat with ivory fur collar.
Cream silk camisole and brown velvet trousers.
Designed for Kate Hudson as Penny Lane
in ALMOST FAMOUS (2000).

JOANNA JOHNSTON

LOVE ACTUALLY was a complex parallel tale of ten love storylines. Director/writer Richard Curtis wanted to project a sense of place about London in the way Woody Allen's MANHATTAN did about New York. Richard's film scripts have a basis in reality, but they usually have an idealistic patina which makes them so popular; however, this work has a darker, more emotional feeling underpinning it. Costume-wise, I would say we were absolutely based in reality, but my challenge was to quickly define and establish each character by his or her clothing. The cast is presented quite quickly on the screen in short scenes, so the production designer Jim Clay and I had to create a strong sense of place and person, so that the audience would quickly identify with them; there was no arc to the characters, so it had to be an immediate identification. I normally work a lot more with color, but on this job I found it was much more about texture and assembly of clothes to make the definition. Contemporary films often depend on delicate and subtle design; it's a very fine line, I think, to hit the right balance. It's easy to either go too far, or not far enough, to get the portrayal just right.

Keira Knightley, as Juliet, was a contemporary, beautiful young woman getting married. Richard said, "I want her to look totally gorgeous, modern and sexy: what about her having a bare tummy in the church?" After talking him out of that, I came up with the proposal of her having layers which unpeeled to reveal different looks. In the church she wears a long, watery, lightweight coat, made in nylon with a train, for the formality of the occasion, then underneath her wedding dress is in a modern layered look with sheerness in her middle section. It is made up of five different fabrics, with the dress being lined in a blush pink, then the middle layer a fine net with clear sequins, then laid on that an asymmetrical short bodice and wrap skirt in a textured lace with silver mesh buckle holding it across at the low side hip. The coat had a trim of fine feathers around the neck, and the overall effect was ivory with a hint of this pink underneath, all very fine and delicate. When you see her leave for her honeymoon, and she is in jeans, a funky cotton coat and little shimmery sequined top, she's urban, casual, funky and lovely. That was certainly the idea.

· FILMOGRAPHY ·

HELLRAISER (1987) · WHO FRAMED ROGER RABBIT (1988) · INDIANA JONES AND THE LAST CRUSADE (1989)
BACK TO THE FUTURE PART II (1989) · BACK TO THE FUTURE PART III (1989) · FAR AND AWAY (1992)
DEATH BECOMES HER (1992) · FORREST GUMP (1994) · FRENCH KISS (1995) · CONTACT (1997)
SAVING PRIVATE RYAN (1998) · THE SIXTH SENSE (1999) · UNBREAKABLE (2000) · CAST AWAY (2000)
ABOUT A BOY (2002) · LOVE ACTUALLY (2003) · POLAR EXPRESS (2004)

Ivory and pastel pink wedding dress of silk, nylon, cotton and feathers. Sequined ivory lace top, wrapped overskirt and pale pink petticoat. Ivory silk coat with feathers. Designed for Keira Knightley as Juliet in LOVE ACTUALLY (2003).

GARY JONES

The longer I do this, the more I realize that the smallest costume detail can turn into an event on screen. In TWO WEEKS NOTICE, Sandra Bullock plays Lucy, a woman who is very politically liberal, who is more comfortable in Birkenstocks than an evening gown. But she needs to attend a charity ball and knows she has to have something appropriate. Sandra and I had originally felt that this might be an opportunity to do a very big dress. But they all either literally looked like prom dresses or she looked like Scarlett O'Hara in GONE WITH THE WIND. So from there we bought about 20 different dresses that might express the right moment in the story. The problem was one dress had the right shape but had the wrong construction; another would look nice up close but needed a more heightened reality. Finally, we were in Soho and scrambling and I just decided to take everything I knew about Sandra and the character and sat down and drew the gown on a napkin in a restaurant.

The idea was her version of a tuxedo, but done as a formal dress – something the character could look her best in but also feel comfortable in. Something that expressed who she really was. The rationale for the elegant black gown was also that the character desired to be the most beautiful she could be to make that entrance overlooking the Brooklyn Bridge. John David Ridge did a wonderful job making the costume based on the napkin design and it all very quickly came together. The other added detail was the red clown nose Lucy wore, since this was a circus charity ball. We always knew the dress had to fit with the nose and, after all, a "tuxedo" looks good with almost everything.

· FILMOGRAPHY ·
THE OTHER SISTER (1999) · THE TALENTED MR. RIPLEY (1999) [A.A. NOMINATION WITH ANN ROTH]
HEARTBREAKERS (2001) · THE PRINCESS DIARIES (2001) · DIVINE SECRETS OF THE YA-YA SISTERHOOD (2002)
TWO WEEKS NOTICE (2002) · SECONDHAND LIONS (2003) · RAISING HELEN (2004)
SPIDER-MAN 2 (2004) · PRINCESS DIARIES 2: THE ROYAL ENGAGEMENT (2004)

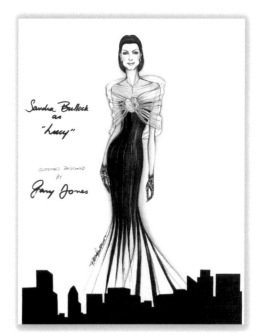

Black silk faille strapless floor-length gown with ivory nylon tulle godets. Ivory silk tulle stole. Worn with red clown nose and black satin shoes. Designed for Sandra Bullock as Lucy Kelson in TWO WEEKS NOTICE (2002).

49

RENÉE EHRLICH KALFUS

The research that really caught my eye for this particular character in CHOCOLAT was some fantastic '50s photography books of rural France by Robert Doisneau and Willie Ronis, which captured the essence of French life. It was a visual reference of a girl in a market from which the director, Lasse Hallström, and I developed Juliette Binoche's character, Vianne Rocher, as an outsider and non-conformist who comes into a very conventional, small community in rural France. Vianne owned a natural sexiness with her high heels, the rich color and sensual shape of her clothes, and the dip of her low-cut deep burgundy red dress, which infuriated these very conventional villagers. Vianne's clothes and accessories were influenced by her exotic travels. She wears this red dress when she makes a chocolate potion that cures the local townspeople from whatever ails them; this candy had a magical psychic power.

She wears a pair of antique earrings from the Paris flea market that reference a much earlier period in her life, and she never changes those. To achieve the silhouette of the period, her undergarment was a very beautifully constructed corset. We found a very old corset maker in Paris who had been making them since the dawn of creation. It was the perfect shade of lingerie nude boned silk, which Juliette was sucked into within an inch of her life. I showed Juliette research of the town she was traveling from, and clothes that represented the kind of a young woman of the time. Research is a good place to start a dialogue with an actor.

Her love interest, Roux, played by Johnny Depp, arrived in the form of another outsider, a riverboat gypsy, and I coordinated their color palette so they could recognize one another instantly as iconoclasts. There certainly was subliminal recognition through the richness of colors and textures. This included Vianne's daughter, who treks around with her from town to town, and who also shares a very similar color palette. The same design collaborators for CHOCOLAT had also worked together on the very subdued film, CIDER HOUSE RULES, which was very specific to its locale of New England. We put our heads together and decided this is just a sexier and a more colorful film.

· FILMOGRAPHY ·
ONCE AROUND (1991) · WHAT'S EATING GILBERT GRAPE (1993) · WITH HONORS (1994)
SAFE PASSAGE (1994) · LET IT BE ME (1995) · DEAD MAN WALKING (1995) · THE EVENING STAR (1996)
ADDICTED TO LOVE (1997) · THE CIDER HOUSE RULES (1999) · SNOW FALLING ON CEDARS (1999)
PAY IT FORWARD (2000) · CHOCOLAT (2000) · THE SHIPPING NEWS (2001)
THE LIFE OF DAVID GALE (2003) · LADDER 49 (2004)

1959-style below knee-length red sheath dress with low-cut scoop neck. Burgundy rose printed cotton of deep green leaves over maroon background. Three-quarter sleeves. Designed for Juliette Binoche as Vianne Rocher in CHOCOLAT (2000).

MICHAEL KAPLAN

I've worked on four films with director David Fincher, and three with Brad Pitt. I love collaborating with them both. Brad has always been very clear about staying true to the character – there's little in the way of frivolity or vanity in his choices. Fincher generally likes a low-key color palatte and never wants the clothing to be noticed or to upstage the characters. This too is usually my approach.

In FIGHT CLUB, however, I felt Tyler Durden (Brad's character), because of his flamboyance and outrageousness, required a stronger stand. I was a bit nervous as to how Brad, and especially Fincher would react to my ideas for the film. When I approached Fincher and asked how far I could go with Tyler, he suprisingly answered, "You can't go too far." Wow! Carte blanche. Brad was cool with that.

In the wardrobe trailer we had Edward Norton's clothes hanging on one side and Brad's directly across. When you walked down the center aisle you couldn't believe these two characters were in the same film. Edward's palette was grey and beige, conservative and just totally, totally boring. You'd fall asleep talking to this person. On the other side of the aisle were scarlets, fuchia, orange yellow and rust; pattern on pattern, outrageous pornographic prints, a shirt emblazened with HUSTLER, a fake-fur coat, etc. I saw Tyler like the male of many animal species, brilliant, proud, cocky and more colorful than the female. Tyler Durden had no income and his wardrobe needed to look as though it came from thrift-shops, which sounds easy, but because of all the action sequences we needed lots of multiples. My job was to produce clothes that looked like one-of-a-kind, second-hand clothes but were produced in quantities. I cracked and broke vintage buttons, sanded and scratched fabrics, I'd even take store tags and staple them to the costumes like they do in thrift shops, and then rip them off just leaving the stapled remnant. One of Brad's favorites was a '70s style leather jacket I designed. I dyed it the color of dried blood which said a lot about the character as well as the film's title.

· FILMOGRAPHY ·

BLADE RUNNER (1982) · FLASHDANCE (1983) · AGAINST ALL ODDS (1984)
AMERICAN DREAMER (1984) · THIEF OF HEARTS (1984) · PERFECT (1985) · CLUE (1985)
TOUGH GUYS DON'T DANCE (1987) · BIG BUSINESS (1988) · COUSINS (1989) · CAT CHASER (1989)
NATIONAL LAMPOON'S CHRISTMAS VACATION (1989) · CURLY SUE (1991) · MALICE (1993) · SEVEN (1995)
THE LONG KISS GOODNIGHT (1996) · THE GAME (1997) · ARMAGEDDON (1998) · FIGHT CLUB (1999)
KEEPING THE FAITH (2000) · PEARL HARBOR (2001) · PANIC ROOM (2002) · TRAPPED (2002)
GIGLI (2003) · MATCHSTICK MEN (2003) · MR. AND MRS. SMITH (2004)

Hip-length dried blood-colored red leather jacket with taupe top-stitching. Polyester double-knit wine trousers. Long sleeve poly/cotton shirt in multi-colored photo print. Designed for Brad Pitt as Tyler Durden in FIGHT CLUB (1999).

CHRISI KARVONIDES-DUSHENKO

The most amazing part of the process of designing BEAUTIFUL was working with director Sally Field. I have not had the luxury of having such a close collaboration with a director very often. To have Sally, whom I could depend on, running down the hall to ask me what the characters' backgrounds would be, how they reached this point in the story, and the best way to show this through costume design, was a dream come true. When I first talked to Sally about designing the opening number for the national beauty pageant in this film, Sally wanted something Americana. We came up with traditional themes from each state for the contestants, very inspired by the '30s...The result was a production number considerably more nostalgic than what they do today.

When Sally and I talked to Minnie Driver about this idea, she revealed a girlhood fantasy of being Pocahontas. We had to dig to find research on the plains Indians of Illinois, where we found beautiful images of Potawatomi Tribe members who wore very ornate beaded costumes. I made ten color Xeroxes of the authentic tribal moccasins and collaged them for a workable beading pattern for the costume. I didn't want the fringed leather dress to look too cowboy-ish, but sexy and curving on her body – appropriate for a beauty contest. I had found an image in a contemporary magazine of beautiful fringe gloves and a skirt that I blended into this creation. Her costume needed to be slightly comical but it also really had to move during the dance number.

My budget was a tenth of any movie costume budget and Minnie required over 20 custom-beaded gowns made for the arc of her pageant career. There were no funds to design a great headdress to match my Indian maiden. Instead, the design details of Minnie's fringe costume were inspired by a fantastic Native American headdress originally made for BATMAN RETURNS and designed by Bob Ringwood. We enhanced and glamorized the original. It was appreciably aged and we had to un-age it. Minnie's costume is one that the general public would just assume to be a rental.

54

· FILMOGRAPHY ·
BEAUTIFUL (2000) · THE GLASS HOUSE (2001) · THE ONE (2001)

Beaded multi-colored fringed leather and suede Native American costume with head-dress, vest, skirt, shoes and gaiters. Trimmed with rabbit fur and marabou feathers. Designed for Minnie Driver as Mona Hibbard in BEAUTIFUL (2000).

JEFFREY KURLAND

The building of characters for a film is the same as building a set or writing a script. In OCEAN'S ELEVEN, Tess (Julia Roberts) is a multi-faceted character. She was trained as an art historian and sold fine art in New York City. After her husband Danny Ocean (George Clooney) is taken to jail, she becomes the girlfriend of a successful Las Vegas casino owner, Terry Benedict (Andy Garcia). The trick was to combine the sophistication of a New York art aficionado with the gaudy, no-expenses-spared world of Las Vegas. I designed Tess's entire wardrobe with these two worlds in mind. Terry Benedict has brought this woman of taste and sophistication into his world to dress it up and give him class. Every time we see Tess, it's an entrance shot. The camera finds her and zeroes in on its target. The audience is meant to be awestruck by her, culminating in her final Vegas ensemble, the "Fight Night Dress." In this dress Tess breaks into a run. I decided on a skin-tight cocktail-length dress, but for practical reasons, I added some swing to the skirt to allow for all of the physical action. Through the solid beadwork on sheer iridescent chiffon, you can see the shadow of her body, keeping it sexy and wearable. At the end of the film, when Tess and Rusty (Brad Pitt) pick Danny up from prison, she greets him in a simple skirt and top; she is far removed from the uber-glamor of Las Vegas.

For OCEAN'S ELEVEN, I pored over books and photos from the '50s, '60s and '70s of Las Vegas, Reno and Atlantic City. We had that style legacy of the original Rat Pack movie, and I wanted to remain true to it. The director, Steven Soderbergh, has extraordinary vision and welcomes the collaboration of a designer. He wanted it larger than real life. My suggestion was the Las Vegas of our fondest memories, the one that doesn't exist anymore. The ideas came from reality. Making it larger than life and still believable is a fine line to tread. With a heightened reality, and having the freedom to create all of the clothes for this film, my imagination and creativity had no boundaries. I was able to tell the story through the costumes precisely as Steven had described it to me, keeping it fresh and original.

· FILMOGRAPHY ·

BROADWAY DANNY ROSE (1984) · PURPLE ROSE OF CAIRO (1985) · HANNAH AND HER SISTERS (1986)
STREETS OF GOLD (1986) · RADIO DAYS (1987) · REVENGE OF THE NERDS II (1987)
SEPTEMBER (1987) · ANOTHER WOMAN (1988) · NEW YORK STORIES-SEGMENT 3 (1989)
CRIMES AND MISDEMEANORS (1989) · QUICK CHANGE (1990) · ALICE (1990) · SHADOWS AND FOG (1992)
THIS IS MY LIFE (1992) · HUSBANDS AND WIVES (1993) · MANHATTAN MURDER MYSTERY (1993)
BULLETS OVER BROADWAY (1994) [A.A. NOMINATION] · MIXED NUTS (1994)
MIGHTY APHRODITE (1995) · EVERYONE SAYS I LOVE YOU (1998) · MY BEST FRIEND'S WEDDING (1997)
LIVING OUT LOUD (1998) · IN DREAMS (1999) · MAN ON THE MOON (1999) · ERIN BROCKOVICH (2000)
WHAT'S THE WORST THAT COULD HAPPEN? (2001) · AMERICA'S SWEETHEARTS (2001)
OCEAN'S ELEVEN (2001) · HIDALGO (2004) · CRIMINAL (2004) · COLLATERAL (2004)

Gold beaded knee-length halter dress of sheer changeable
silk chiffon with bugle beads and mirrors. Gold leather
knee-length coat with bronze tree-print lining.
Designed for Julia Roberts as Tess Ocean
in OCEAN'S ELEVEN (2001).

DAN
LESTER

THE CORE is an updated version of JOURNEY TO THE CENTER OF THE EARTH. Delroy Lindo's character, Dr. Ed "Braz" Brazzleton, has found a way to drill through to the center of the earth, and my challenge was to create a suit that could get the crew outside the ship into the molten earth. Jon Amiel, the director, wanted the design to be industrial, yet a suit the audience would recognize – not Sci-Fi. We wanted to sell the idea that the fabric was technically advanced and could bear the intense heat. After a great deal of research, we found a fabric called "asteroid." It was created by the aerospace industry and used light interference technology that splits colors into different shades, depending on the angle of the light source. The suits needed to follow the contours of the actors' bodies, be convincing as working garments, yet not be as oversized and clumsy as the NASA suits. We definitely didn't want that skintight science-fiction thing. Particularly, I liked the old Russian cosmonaut suits. The typical NASA space outfit is a solid color. A Russian suit has the same shape, but under and around the shoulders, knees, and joints there is contrasting color; it looks cool.

Our job as costume designers is to communicate to the audience who they're seeing, and to help the director move the story along. We sculpted the helmet and set lights inside the helmet to make sure that the camera could see the actors' faces. Philip Harrison, the production designer, created the interior of the ship in very cool tones. As a contrast, Brazzleton was entirely dressed in a warm palette (other than the thermal suit) because he always worked around the earth. This particular thermal suit reacted well to the different gels that the cinematographer, John Lindley, used. When there was a lot of reflected red and gold light from the heat on the ship, it looked great. Phyllis Therburn-Moffet aged the suit in three stages, using both heat and paint. As Braz enters the reactor core, his suit melts around him and starts to warp, like a Coke bottle in the desert. As Brazzleton leans into the wall, the shape of the suit changes, and the silver blackens into charcoal as the audience watches him melt to death.

58

· FILMOGRAPHY ·
TIME COP (1994) · SUDDEN DEATH (1995) · SAVAGE (1995) · THE RELIC (1997)
SPAWN (1997) · I STILL KNOW WHAT YOU DID LAST SUMMER (1998) · THE CORE (2003)

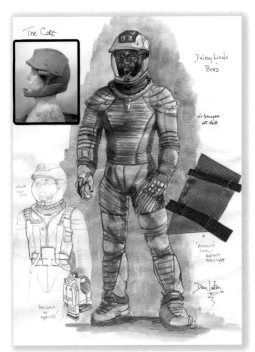

Silver *Asteroid* fabric space suit, with olive green
tape binding. Gloves, boots and helmet.
Designed for Delroy Lindo as Dr. Ed 'Braz'
Brazzleton in THE CORE (2003).

JUDIANNA MAKOVSKY

My very first meeting in England was with director Chris Columbus, the producer David Heyman and author J.K. Rowling. I had only one conversation with J.K. Rowling. One of my questions for her was: How did she see Dumbledore? She replied she thought he was a bit of a clotheshorse and had large flowing robes, which we then determined to be sort of Renaissance after looking at a few pieces of research I had brought to the meeting. That was all the info I really ever got. At that point, the actors had not been cast, though we knew Chris wanted Richard Harris. I designed from the very few descriptions in the book. I tried to have a sense of humor with Dumbledore, with that patchworky hat, like those old 19th century Arthur Rackham paintings. I had drawn a little sketch that everybody agreed they liked. I have to admit, I've never looked at so many different periods for one project. Each character was based on a different period, and it got a little confusing after a while to keep it all straight; it's one thing when you do a film and you have to learn all about one period. For HARRY POTTER we researched everything from medieval sources to images of a Mexican surrealist painter.

Most of the garments are based on academic robes, and no matter what period, you'd recognize who's the teacher and who's the student. If you read the book closely, most everything is described as either purple or green, and that's where I started from. Dumbledore's robe is fully embroidered and has a beautiful fake fur collar embossed with a Renaissance design stamped in gold leaf made by an Irish textile artist. The overrobe is silk overlayed with velvet and embroidered in Bonaz (or English) technique. The design was based on a Celtic door in Scotland. Dumbledore has a beautiful belt described in the book. I interpreted it as a gold-stamped belt with a Celtic buckle with inlaid stones that I had cast by a jewelry artist in England. Production Designer Stuart Craig and I tried to keep Hogwarts' world elegant, simple, clean and a little silly. I also worked very closely with the set decorator Stephenie McMillan for the colors and fabrics she was using.

· FILMOGRAPHY ·

GARDENS OF STONE (1987) · BIG (1988) · LOST ANGELS (1989) · REVERSAL OF FORTUNE (1990)
SIX DEGREES OF SEPARATION (1993) · THE REF (1994) · THE SPECIALIST (1994)
THE QUICK AND THE DEAD (1995) · A LITTLE PRINCESS (1995) · WHITE SQUALL (1996)
LOLITA (1997) · DEVIL'S ADVOCATE (1997) · GREAT EXPECTATIONS (1998)
PLEASANTVILLE (1998) [A.A. NOMINATION] · PRACTICAL MAGIC (1998) · GLORIA (1999)
FOR THE LOVE OF THE GAME (1999) · THE LEGEND OF BAGGER VANCE (2000)
HARRY POTTER AND THE SORCERER'S STONE (2001) [A.A. NOMINATION]
SEABISCUIT (2003) [A.A. NOMINATION] · NATIONAL TREASURE (2004)

Dark burgundy/brown changeable silk wizards robe appliquéd
with velvet Celtic motifs. Dark brown faux beaver fur collar
and cuffs stamped with square Renaissance designs.
Designed for Richard Harris as Albus Dumbledore in HARRY
POTTER AND THE SORCERER'S STONE (2001).

61

MONA MAY

My costume designs for Rob Minkoff's HAUNTED MANSION needed to overcome some very unusual and challenging problems. After researching the many past films in which ghosts had been photographed, we decided that the ghosts should have a very organic look and be in themselves an effect, not just a computer-generated image. The costumes needed to glow and at the same time give the appearance that the fabric was still real, with aging, rips and flowing movement. During camera tests to find the right effect, Remi Adefarasin, our Director of Photography, suggested using Scotchlite™, a reflective product that all of us have seen on road signs, running shoes and sports wear. This material comes as microscopic glass beads in powder form. I believed that this would be the right product, but how to apply it, on what color fabric, and how it would affect the fabric? All had to be tested. More important, how would it look on film?

For our first test, we mixed the powder with paint in various strengths and brushed it on black fabric. When we viewed it, the glowing effect worked but the costumes disappeared, so we had to try a different approach. We then used the Scotchlite on new costumes made with brighter fabric to make the outline stronger. For each costume, varying degrees of saturation of the powder and paint had to be adjusted to get the right brightness. We also decided to outline the clothes' natural folds and silhouette with the paint mixture. This technique, along with a special lighting rig created by Remi, gave HAUNTED MANSION costumes that glowed more organically, and an effect that could be customized for each costume and character's personality.

Once it was seen how well this effect would work, I went to work creating a complete sub-department of seamstresses, painters and agers. Each of the 60 costumes for the ghosts in the graveyard scene were hand-painted and designed with this effect, using a variety of techniques (i.e. lace, plaid, patterns, silhouettes). In the end, each ghost had a unique, sparkly diamond-like glow, that produced a very eerie mood and enhanced the film.

· FILMOGRAPHY ·

3 NINJAS (1992) · VALHALLA (1992) · HOUSE IV (1992) · BEST OF THE BEST II (1993) · CLUELESS (1995)
HIGH SCHOOL HIGH (1996) · ROMY AND MICHELE'S HIGH SCHOOL REUNION (1997)
THE WEDDING SINGER (1998) · A NIGHT AT THE ROXBURY (1998) · 8MM (1999)
NEVER BEEN KISSED (1999) · LOSER (2000) · STUART LITTLE 2 (2002)
THE MASTER OF DISGUISE (2002) · EASY (2003) · THE HAUNTED MANSION (2003)

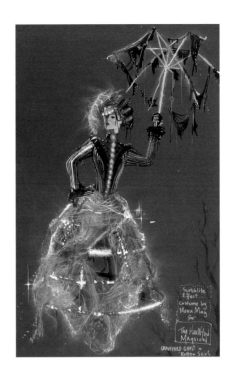

19th-century fuchsia and black striped bodice, purple-gray and fuchsia distressed hoop-skirt. Ghost costume hand painted with Scotchlite™ reflective paint which is only visible in the dark. Designed for ghost character in THE HAUNTED MANSION (2003).

63

GRACIELA
MAZON

This black, red and lace dress was based on a religious painting of a virgin from 1760, which had a strong flavor of the mysticism of Spanish culture. This intense visual image had a contrast of colors, textures, and styles. There was fruit hanging from the ruffles made with black and red beads, and the skirt was embroidered with brilliantly shimmering moons and stars. The character of Elena (Catherine Zeta-Jones) was a very passionate person and I wanted to transmit that extremely romantic essence. The mood of this gown played very much to the natural strength of a traditional bullfighter costume.

After reading the script of ZORRO, I discussed Elena's character with the director, Martin Campbell, who was very respectful of my ideas. Elena was not an isolated woman; she wanted to participate in her community and had strong beliefs in freedom and justice. She wears this costume at a party where she meets Alejandro (Antonio Banderas), the young Zorro, for a second time. They have a passionate dance; a mix of tango and traditional music and it was possible to create some fire between them with this vibrant dress.

With Martin's approval, I followed the arc of Zorro's character with his costume. After I read the script, I proposed a rough Zorro, a Zorro with thorns and texture who was a guerriero fighting for his people and for justice. My feeling was that the costume needed to echo the character development of Zorro, first as a student in preparation, then as the master himself. Martin and I had a meeting with the studio and they liked my idea, but they wanted the classic black Zorro. My solution worked well. When Zorro is in training to his teacher Diego de la Vega (Anthony Hopkins), he is in a coarse brown palette. Then, when he is becomes ready to take the responsibility and the role of Zorro from his mentor, he finally earns the elegant black Zorro costume.

· FILMOGRAPHY ·
MIROSLAVA (1993) · THE QUEEN OF THE NIGHT (1994) · DESPERADO (1995)
FROM DUSK TILL DAWN (1996) · THE MASK OF ZORRO (1998) · CRAZY IN ALABAMA (1999)
VERTICAL LIMIT (2000) · SPY KIDS 2: ISLAND OF LOST DREAMS (2002) · ONCE UPON A TIME IN MEXICO (2003)

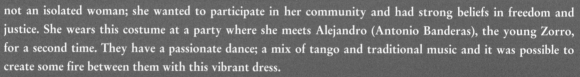

Mid 19th-century black and red ruffled ball gown of velvet
and silk crepe. Trimmed with gold lace, and beaded red
and black fruit. Ivory underskirt embroidered
with shimmering moon and stars.
Designed for Catherine Zeta-Jones as Elena
in THE MASK OF ZORRO (1998).

ELLEN
MIROJNICK

Director Adrian Lyne shoots an urban movie in a specific kind of humanistic way. He changes his design team every so often, but basically keeps the same sensibility around him. When you work for Adrian, he really doesn't care what the garments are, but you have to work doubly hard to make them disappear so that they just drape over the actors' bodies, allowing the body language of the actors to speak the movie. It's really using color and form to convey the message, as opposed to a garment itself. Adrian is such a sensory director to work for that he won't push something that he doesn't really feel is organic. He is in tune with human frailty and humanness in the film UNFAITHFUL.

Richard Gere signed on to play the role of Edward, but in Adrian's mind Richard had a preconceived image. I had already worked with Richard on another film, and we had a friendly relationship. Adrian took me aside and said, "I don't want him to be Richard Gere." I said, "That's fine Adrian. Would you like him to be like you?" "No-no-no. But yes, but no." He was very embarrassed. In watching Adrian and Richard try to have a dialogue about this character, Adrian, without himself knowing it, was asking Edward to dress like Adrian. The character was a lawyer, but he was going to be a comfortable lawyer – successful, but with stylish British schlumpiness: baggy and unselfconscious. Richard was only going to wear work boots, corduroys, textural fabrics and maybe he'd have a vest. I suggested this to Adrian and he said, "Well that sounds fine darling. Show it to me." And I showed it to him and said, "You know Richard called me up and he had this idea to look like you." That was a total lie, but Adrian bought it. He said, "That's what I want then…He does? He wants to look like me?" And I told Richard the opposite story. And Richard bought it and the two of them fell in love. They had the biggest crush on each other, and the character worked!

· FILMOGRAPHY ·

FRENCH QUARTER (1977) · FAME (1980) · RECKLESS (1984) · THE FLAMINGO KID (1984)
REMO WILLIAMS: THE ADVENTURE BEGINS (1985) · NOBODY'S FOOL (1986) · FATAL ATTRACTION (1987)
WALL STREET (1987) · COCKTAIL (1988) · TALK RADIO (1988) · BLACK RAIN (1989) · ALWAYS (1989)
NARROW MARGIN (1990) · JACOB'S LADDER (1990) · SWITCH (1991) · MOBSTERS (1991)
BASIC INSTINCT (1992) · CHAPLIN (1992) · CLIFFHANGER (1993) · INTERSECTION (1994) · SPEED (1994)
SHOWGIRLS (1995) · STRANGE DAYS (1995) · MULHOLLAND FALLS (1996) · TWISTER (1996)
THE GHOST AND THE DARKNESS (1996) · FACE/OFF (1997) · STARSHIP TROOPERS (1997)
A PERFECT MURDER (1998) · THE HAUNTING (1999) · MICKEY BLUE EYES (1999) · HOLLOW MAN (2000)
WHAT WOMEN WANT (2000) · ONE NIGHT AT MCCOOL'S (2001) · AMERICA'S SWEETHEARTS (2001)
RAT RACE (2001) · DON'T SAY A WORD (2001) · UNFAITHFUL (2002) · IT RUNS IN THE FAMILY (2003)
TWISTED (2004) · THE CHRONICLES OF RIDDICK (2004)

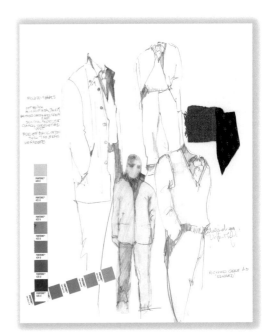

Black micro-fiber jacket and cotton twill trousers. Cotton flannel shirt with charcoal gray wool vest and gray silk foulard tie. Designed for Richard Gere as Edward 'Ed' Sumner in UNFAITHFUL (2002).

6 7

ABIGAIL MURRAY

In RUNAWAY JURY Dustin Hoffman plays Wendell Rohr, a lawyer who is not from the South but has lived there for many years. Every character always comes from the words on the page of the script – it is there somewhere. Hopefully, the director has an "interpretation," a vision, as film is a real collaboration. To research Dustin's character I went to New Orleans where the story was set. I sat in several courtrooms and talked with some fascinating, flamboyant lawyers. I enmeshed myself in the legal world. I gave Gary Fleder, the director, all the visual tools I had collected: photographs, sketches, fabrics and even sample garments (new, used or antique). Instead of a conventional suit, I chose to put Dustin in a jacket, vest, pants, shirt, all totally mismatched, but all in the same warm tones so that no one could really tell. It gave him a look that made him "court presentable" but a little different. Costumes should enhance the character, never overcome. Dustin is a joy to work with and when I showed him a picture of where I wanted to go with this character, he said, "Great idea. I'll stand in the fittings and shut my mouth as you have really done your homework." He had five different "suits," designed and made, all just five uncoordinated outfits mixed and matched in a particular way.

For Gene Hackman, also a joy to work with, the director said, "When I think of Rankin Fitch, all I see is the devil." I designed a lean mean money-making machine who always had a touch of red. It could be in his cufflink, tie, or stripe in his suit. He was a dark, slim, tall, menacing-looking character playing against Dustin's very warm, light, Wendall Rohr.

The jury consisted of twelve people all with individual stories in the novel, but not in the script. I had to quickly give them some kind of identity; i.e. the woman who was a potter who loved colors, a food manager who liked his clothes loose and comfortable – they each needed their own wardrobe from their life. And the audience had to visually differentiate them according to their look.

· FILMOGRAPHY ·
BLOODHOUNDS OF BROADWAY (1989) · TREMORS (1990) · AIRBORNE (1993)
THINGS TO DO IN DENVER WHEN YOU'RE DEAD (1995) · THE PROPRIETOR (1996)
KISS THE GIRLS (1997) · FOR RICHER OR POORER (1997) · DOGMA (1999) · SCREAM 3 (2000)
IMPOSTOR (2002) · MASKED AND ANONYMOUS (2003) · RUNAWAY JURY (2003)

Wool hounds-tooth sport coat with patterned wool vest.
Blue striped dress shirt and pinstriped ivory trousers.
Brown wingtip spectator shoes and suspenders
decorated with the scales of justice.
Designed for Dustin Hoffman as Wendell Rohr
in RUNAWAY JURY (2003).

RUTH MYERS

I approached NICHOLAS NICKELBY knowing that there was rapport with the director, Douglas McGrath. The novel was set in 1840 and we pushed it 25 years later into the mid-Victorian Industrial Revolution era. Because that time period is one of my favorites, I had a huge amount of research of my own; I was inspired by all those wonderful Victorian paintings. The color palette I used was primarily monochromatic except for the colorful splash of the theatrical players, where I used as my reference the Victorian Pollack Toy Theater prints. Doug ended up using a Pollack print for the credits, so they became very resonant stylistically. Although I worked within the constraints of the period, I was extravagant with the designs of the theatrical troupe – as they would have been.

We designed and made perhaps 90% of the principle costumes. I particularly enjoyed designing this specific character, as Barry Humphreys was playing a woman, and he's a man who's been pretty convincing playing women. Barry arrived from Australia only four days before he was on camera and he came straight from the airport to his first fitting. There were probably four or five changes. His costume was based on a very specific corset, which was boned, padded, pushed and pulled to get that Victorian shape. I had very good petticoats made, gloves, hose, and the most beautiful purple boots with red heels. We made perfect Victorian bonnets suitably plumed and decorated. Barry was adorable from top to toe. Because it was a low-budget film, we did not have the money for expensive fabrics, although I used velvet, chenille, plush and silk and any original trim that I could find. We also painted many of the decorations. Some painting was made to look like embroidery, and since I couldn't find the right scale or anything as purely Victorian as I wanted, this worked perfectly. We didn't have enough money but we managed to do it. I know that I did one cloak where I painted the entire border. It was divine.

· FILMOGRAPHY ·

THE ROMANTIC ENGLISHWOMAN (1975) · THE ADVENTURE OF SHERLOCK HOLMES' SMARTER BROTHER (1975)
THE WORLD'S GREATEST LOVER (1977) · MAGIC (1978) · THE MAIN EVENT (1979)
AND JUSTICE FOR ALL (1979) · ALTERED STATES (1980) · CANNERY ROW (1982) · THE WOMAN IN RED (1984)
PLENTY (1985) · HAUNTED HONEYMOON (1986) · THE ACCIDENTAL TOURIST (1988) ·
BERT RIGBY, YOU'RE A FOOL (1989) · BLAZE (1989) · THE RUSSIA HOUSE (1990) · THE MARRYING MAN (1991)
THE ADDAMS FAMILY (1991) [A.A. NOMINATION] · MR. SATURDAY NIGHT (1992) · THE FIRM (1993)
I.Q. (1994) · HOW TO MAKE AN AMERICAN QUILT (1995) · EMMA (1996) [A.A. NOMINATION]
L.A. CONFIDENTIAL (1997) · A THOUSAND ACRES (1997) · DEEP IMPACT (1998) · CRADLE WILL ROCK (1999)
COMPANY MAN (2000) · CENTER STAGE (2001) · PROOF OF LIFE (2000) · IRIS (2001)
THE FOUR FEATHERS (2002) · NICHOLAS NICKLEBY (2002) · ELLA ENCHANTED (2004)
CONNIE AND CARLA (2004) · BEYOND THE SEA (2004)

Late 19th-century orange silk bodice with teal velvet flowered cape and burgundy cotton skirt. Coral bonnet and purple boots with red heels. Designed for Barry Humphries as Mrs. Crummles in NICHOLAS NICKLEBY (2002).

DEBORAH
NADOOLMAN

In the musical comedy BLUES BROTHERS 2000, hip-hop artist Erykah Badu played Queen Musette, a ravishing 200-year-old Cajun voodoo witch with devastating magic powers. Her club was a spicy operatic mélange of styles, from 'Louis Hotel' to House of Blues, redolent with magnolias and swamp moss. Sometimes costume research can simply be experiential. For example, Musette's security force, the Ton Ton Macoute, were dressed exactly as I remember in Port au Prince in the '60s. They wore aviator glasses, blue chambray shirts, straw cowboy hats, boots and narrow jeans. We deliberately cast the tallest, thinnest dancers for a zombie chorus line. Queen Musette provided the heat and magnetic center of the last scenes in the film; the landing place for a mixed bag of low-life musicians and recidivists. While she croons a rendition of "Funky Nassau," Musette turns the noncompliant Elwood (Dan Aykroyd), and Mack (John Goodman), into zombies while the rest of their band accompanies her in white dinner jackets. Director John Landis brightened the mood of this sequel, and during our many film collaborations has spoiled me with his trust. The style of the Blues Brothers films reflected the time in which they were made: the grim deterioration of the cities in the '70s, and the Clintonian optimism of the '90s.

General Henri Christophe liberated Haiti from Napoleon. Christophe crowned himself emperor and created a short-lived royal court mimicking French aristocracy. Freely associating voodoo, late 18th century French court costume, and the Caribbean, I designed sky high twisted dreadlocks for Eryka, resembling a powdered, Marie Antoinette wig. Instead of curls tumbling over Eryka's shoulders, there were long uneven dreadlocks hanging down her back. I channeled romantic Meissen harlequins for her polonaise gown of red, yellow and black African cotton batik encrusted with bugle beads and Swarovski crystals. Jewelry designer Ezmaralda Gordon, who also co-designed the regalia for COMING TO AMERICA, collaborated on a pirate treasure chest necklace, with topaz and black pearl drops. Erykah Badu, to her great credit, saw the sketch and instantly loved the idea of the early French-African aristocracy in Haiti, and Queen Musette as a relic and survivor from that time.

· FILMOGRAPHY ·

THE KENTUCKY FRIED MOVIE (1977) · ANIMAL HOUSE (1978) · 1941 (1979) · THE BLUES BROTHERS (1980)
RAIDERS OF THE LOST ARK (1981) · AN AMERICAN WEREWOLF IN LONDON (1981)
TRADING PLACES (1983) · INTO THE NIGHT (1985) · SPIES LIKE US (1985) · THREE AMIGOS! (1986)
COMING TO AMERICA (1988) [A.A. NOMINATION] · NOTHING BUT TROUBLE (1991)
OSCAR (1991) · INNOCENT BLOOD (1992) · THE STUPIDS (1996) · MAD CITY (1997)
BLUES BROTHERS 2000 (1998) · SUSAN'S PLAN (1998)

Late 18th-century polonaise gown of hand-painted African
Batik cotton in a gold, red and black harlequin pattern.
Embellished with glass bugle beads and Swarovski crystals.
Designed for Erykah Badu as Queen Mousette in
BLUES BROTHERS 2000 (1998).

DANIEL ORLANDI

It's 1963, but it's Hollywood/Doris Day 1963. For DOWN WITH LOVE, we went for the authentic, unrealistic look of those movies, and what working women wore for that Hollywood back-lot soundstage look. We wanted that Technicolor sparkling candy-colored look in sets, with costumes that matched. Peyton Reid, the director, wanted the costumes to be like another character in the movie. The girls walk in, the music starts and they show off their fabulous outfits. After an outrageous entrance, they could take off their top layer and play the scene in one of those sixties kind of sleek, simple dresses. I presented Renée Zellweger thirty sketches and we made all of the clothes and had her fittings, and we changed almost nothing. This dress is Renée's rhumba dress from the dating montage. It's a pale Jordan almond orchid color, hand-embroidered, sequined sheath. It's got clear and A.B. sequins over the lilac and an ostrich feather hem. She can walk in the highest, pointiest heels because she's an actress playing the part, and she did it. It's something innate, clothes don't wear her.

The most challenging thing was that we wanted it to be fun and fresh, but we didn't want the actors to look ridiculous, campy or stupid. They all jumped right in and they weren't afraid of the look, they didn't let it scare them. I designed everything so that the proportions, necklines, and color were what I thought would be best for them. The actors put on the costumes and they fit. The proportion was perfect and it made them look taller and thinner. The production designer, Andrew Laws, and I worked so closely together that the pink of Renée's suit is the exact pink of her couch, and the red of David Hyde Pierce's vest is the exact color of his wall and his office. Because his office was across from mine we'd look at each other's swatches and research, and look at a chair and look at a dress and look at fabric, and the producers would come in and it was just so much fun!

74

· FILMOGRAPHY ·
QUICK (1993) · THE FAN (1996) · ROCKET MAN (1997) · FLAWLESS (1999) · MEET THE PARENTS (2000)
PHONE BOOTH (2002) · KANGAROO JACK (2003) · DOWN WITH LOVE (2003)
MY BOSS'S DAUGHTER (2003) · THE ALAMO (2004)

Hand sequined sleeveless sheath dress of orchid-colored silk chiffon with ostrich feather hem. Silk taffeta cape with feathers and bow. Designed for Renée Zellweger as Barbara Novak in DOWN WITH LOVE (2003).

RENEE ZELLWEGER

DOWN WITH LOVE
"RHUMBA"
DRESS

Orlandi 2003

BETH PASTERNAK

ARARAT is an emotional and heartfelt film that carries the memory and pain of the Armenian genocide across generations. The director, Atom Egoyan, is Armenian and it was his goal not just to render a historical retelling but also to illustrate how the anguish of the genocide has affected the psychic life of the contemporary Armenian community. The film takes place in the city of Van in 1915. Due to Van's position as a Pan Asian destination, I was able to access a tremendous cross section of cultural life.

My research followed many paths and contained a potent mix of Persian, Russian, Asian, and American influences. The script called for three levels of the period's social strata – civilian (Armenian village), missionary (Christian) and military (Turkish and Armenian Fedayee). I am indebted to Ruth Thomasian of "Project Save" for allowing me access to her historical photographs. The 'ghosts' contained within these photographs became the basis for the recreation of villages and their missing inhabitants. The Armenian Library Museum also was helpful in allowing me to reproduce their authentic museum-quality costumes. Finally, the Houghton Library at Harvard contributed to my research with its collection of overseas Missionary diaries.

Armed with an abundance of excellent and exciting research, the trick of course became how to harness these wonderful materials within the production's limitations of time and budget. The process of creation included silk-screening printed textiles onto textured fabric to create the illusion of what we were seeing in the woven archival costumes. It was time consuming to figure out the scale, color and patterns on paper. We experimented a lot with resist printing, which involves taking color out of the fabric to reproduce complicated embroidery patterns. We made between five and six hundred costumes. It was an intense race against the clock to get finished on time. To stay on track, we came to depend upon our Costume Bible, which contained our research of Eastern and Western culture and the details of Turkish and Armenian Fedayee military uniforms. The palette was divided between the historic and contempory parts of the story. Whereas each actor in the contemporary scenes had his own color, the historic palette was represented by the region itself. Spice colors, natural and muted, dominated.

It was an emotional subject to recreate. The period was of course dominated by death and starvation and I continually found it unsettling to be confronted by beauty in such a wilderness of pain. The process of costuming women and children to create the illusion that they were starving was overwhelming at times. I had a crew of twenty and we all went through quite an emotional ride together. The starvation march costumes were worn largely by background performers from the Armenian Community. Once in costume they were able to access their shared past and consequently became invested in the emotion of those who think they are being led to Refugee Camps only to find out that they being led into the middle of the desert to starve to death. The fabric utilized on this march was muted eggshell blue cotton, dyed a number of times, painted and finally burnt out using potassium promagenite. My collaborator in this technique was the British-trained breakdown artist, Trelawnie Meade. She was diligent in ensuring that everything looked just right.

· FILMOGRAPHY ·

HOSTILE TAKEOVER (1988) · THE TOP OF HIS HEAD (1989) · WHITE ROOM (1990) ·
FRIENDS, LOVERS & LUNATICS (1989) · MASALA (1991) · GIANT STEPS (1992) · THE GATE II: TRESPASSERS (1992)
I LOVE A MAN IN UNIFORM (1993) · DANCE ME OUTSIDE (1995) · CURTIS'S CHARM (1995)
THE SWEET HEREAFTER (1997) · DIRTY WORK (1998) · NEW JERSEY TURNPIKES (1999) · COMMITTED (2000)
SAINT JUDE (2000) · KNOCKAROUND GUYS (2001) · ARARAT (2002) · A HOME AT THE END OF THE WORLD (2004)

1910 Armenian gray-blue cotton shroud with brown burnout created using potassium permanganate. Spray dyed with highlights and lowlights. Designed for Armenian woman from starvation march in ARARAT (2002).

77

KAREN PATCH

Since HOW TO LOSE A GUY IN 10 DAYS took place in the specific world of New York fashion journalism, I met with editors at both Allure and Vogue. I went to Condé Nast and hung out in the cafeteria to get a real sense of how they put themselves together and how young professionals that weren't in high-paying jobs could afford to dress fashionably. Fashion people are given a lot of gifts from designers who want to have their things seen. The way that they put things together using vintage pieces, mixing it up with a jacket from the Gap and a Prada bag, that's how I started building the wardrobe for Andie Anderson, played by Kate Hudson. This was one of the few movies where using Seventh Avenue designer fashions might be appropriate. When I went in to meet with director Donald Petrie, I brought my sketches and he was completely open to my ideas. Kate and I were completely on the same page.

Mathew McConaughey plays an ad account executive named Ben Barry. He's invited her to a formal party on short notice and she arrives in a borrowed dress. The CEO of a Harry Winston kind of company whom Mathew is courting places a necklace on Kate Hudson. As scripted she wears an 82-karat diamond; I went into Harry Winston and chose a yellow diamond. A lot of people don't think blondes look great in yellow, but I love blondes in yellow and there was no question that it looked great on her. I designed about a half dozen different colored tops that we camera tested with the necklace, and the yellow was just amazing. The gown is a bias cut '30s style cut deep in the back and held together by high crisscross straps with a very slight train. The color palette at the party was very controlled. Everyone in the background was in subtle colors, all the men are in black tie with all the women fairly colorless in gray, beige, or black, so that Kate would stand out in that room.

· FILMOGRAPHY ·

CHATTAHOOCHEE (1989) · THE BIG PICTURE (1989) · MIDNIGHT FEAR (1990) · BRIGHT ANGEL (1991)
MY GIRL (1991) · ASPEN EXTREME (1993) · HOMEWARD BOUND: THE INCREDIBLE JOURNEY (1993)
BOTTLE ROCKET (1996) · RUSHMORE (1998) · SIMPATICO (1999) · THE ROYAL TENENBAUMS (2001)
HOW TO LOSE A GUY IN 10 DAYS (2003) · THE SCHOOL OF ROCK (2003)

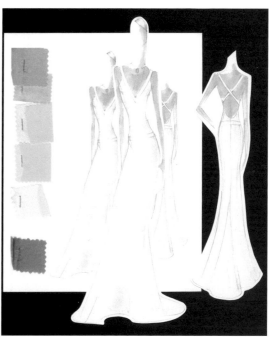

Yellow silk charmeuse bias-cut floor-length gown with train.
Deep V-front and wide spaghetti straps which cross at back.
Designed for Kate Hudson as Andie Anderson in
HOW TO LOSE A GUY IN 10 DAYS (2003).

GABRIELLA PESCUCCI

It was the first time I had worked with the director Michael Hoffman. Although I hadn't read the script, I knew the story of A MIDSUMMER NIGHT'S DREAM. I try to wait until I meet the principal actors before I design because I need time for my costume ideas to germinate, as day by day they get better. The first part of the film was a realistic portrayal of the period, very elegant with no ostentation and I stuck very close to historical accuracy. The second part is complete fantasy. There was not much preparation time, but I did all the research and assembled it and created samples for the director. The first part of the film is at the beginning of the 19th-century when we see Titania, Queen of the Fairies, in her world inside the forest. I used very light colors for her costumes, reflecting the colors of the water and the forest.

After screen tests I often try to improve my designs. Not all the costumes were 'set in stone' before shooting began; I designed and made some during the shooting weeks. I always try to use original accessories, e.g. lace, embroidery, collars and cuffs that I find in markets and specialist shops, and I made and rented every costume from my base at Tirelli Costumes in Rome. The film was not shot in continuity; therefore I had to consider the aging process of each costume. I always have a very strong collaboration with Hair and Makeup, because every department is equally important to create a role for an actor.

I like to approach designing costumes for a period movie with an open mind, and allow myself to take every avenue into each historic era. To research how to best represent a period through costumes, I'll look at paintings from that time. Before 1850 there was no photography, and I use paintings for my research; they're an endless source of inspiration. Each movie gives me a different emotion and each period suggests to me different things. Sometimes when I am in a museum and I look at a picture I see an accessory that truly inspires me, and I try to recreate that piece for my character.

· FILMOGRAPHY ·

I Sette Fratelli Cervi (1967) · Many Wars Ago (1970) · Tis Pity She's a Whore (1971)
The Driver's Seat (1974) · The Divine Nymph (1976) · The Inheritance (1978)
Orchestra Rehearsal (1978) · City of Women (1980) · Three Brothers (1981)
Passion of Love (1981) · That Night in Varennes (1982) · Once upon a Time in America (1984)
Orfeo (1985) · The Name of the Rose (1986) · The Family (1987)
The Adventures of Baron Munchausen (1988) [a.a. nomination] · Splendor (1988)
Haunted Summer (1988) · What Time Is It? (1989) · Indochine (1992)
The Age of Innocence (1993) [a.a. winner] · The Scarlet Letter (1995)
Albergo Roma (1996) · Dangerous Beauty (1998) · Les Miserables (1998)
Cousin Bette (1998) · A Midsummer Night's Dream (1999) · Time Regained (1999)
Secret Passage (2002) · Perdutoamor (2003) · Van Helsing (2004)

Sheer Fortuny-pleated empire waist
turquoise/aqua/ivory/gold gown with
beaded tassels and chenille embroidery.
Designed for Michelle Pfeiffer as Titania
in WILLIAM SHAKESPEARE'S
A MIDSUMMER NIGHT'S DREAM (1999).

81

JOSEPH PORRO

I knew SHANGHAI NOON would be a challenge due to the huge variety of costumes I had to design and assemble. What was both scary and exciting was designing the Imperial Court of the Forbidden City. Due to budget constraints, it would be impossible to make these richly embroidered court robes within our budget in America, or in Canada where we were shooting. So I contacted James Acheson, designer of THE LAST EMPEROR, and asked if any of his pieces from that film were available as rental stock. They had all been left in Beijing, so I visited Beijing Studios' wardrobe department. The wardrobe people lived and worked in the same building under very Spartan conditions. All my hopes were dashed when I looked at their stock. Most of the clothes were poor polyester reproductions; where were Jim's costumes from THE LAST EMPEROR? Apparently they had been selling them out the back door for years.

Even more frustrating was that they had one standard women's Imperial Court costume, which was used for a three or four hundred year period. They would insist, "This is what a lady of the court would wear," and I would counter, "Well, no... that's not true." They thought I was crazy until I showed them historical photographs. I now had to quickly design and make the 300 Chinese court costumes for the interiors, more than 500 for the exterior shots, and make it work within my budget.

Through Jackie Chan's contacts in Beijing, we began having my designs for him made, but when we were only three days away from shooting we heard they were having lots of problems, and the costs would be a little higher. I ended up paying twenty times their original estimate! But now there was a bigger problem: I couldn't personally go back to Beijing and find a new manufacturer. Finally it came to me: AN OPERA HOUSE. Chinese Opera uses very traditional designs and embroideries. Only who could I trust as my middleman who wouldn't rob me blind?

I enlisted the help of my cousin, who is in medical supplies in Beijing. I said, "How would you like to get into the movie business?" He thought I was absolutely insane. I sent him itemized, detailed sketches, fabric swatches and photographs of the period and said, "Can you make this happen for me?" And he did.

· FILMOGRAPHY ·

MEET THE APPLEGATES (1991) · THE PERFECT WEAPON (1991) · KICKBOXER 2: THE ROAD BACK (1991)
DOUBLE IMPACT (1991) · UNIVERSAL SOLIDER (1992) · SHADOW OF THE WOLF (1992)
SUPER MARIO BROS. (1993) · TOMBSTONE (1993) · STARGATE (1994)
MIGHTY MORPHIN POWER RANGERS: THE MOVIE (1995) · THE QUEST (1996) · INDEPENDENCE DAY (1996)
MAXIMUM RISK (1996) · DEEP RISING (1998) · HOMEGROWN (1998) · GODZILLA (1998)
THE THIRTEENTH FLOOR (1999) · STUART LITTLE (1999) · SHANGHAI NOON (2000)
EQUILIBRIUM (2002) BLINDNESS (2003) · ULTRAVIOLET (2004)

19th-century Chinese aristocratic man's court dress.
Yellow silk garment with embroidered dragons
and auspicious symbols over a blue ocean.
Designed for Sherman Chao as Emperor's Cousin
in SHANGHAI NOON (2000).

ANTHONY POWELL

The great Disney villain Cruella DeVil, played by Glenn Close, was already established and the sequel 102 DALMATIONS begins with Cruella in jail. She's been undergoing aversion therapy, and is now terribly sweet and loves small animals. Naturally, during the course of the film she turns back into the old Cruella, but for the first half, she's a new, adorable Cruella. It was terribly difficult to work out ideas that would hint at her true evil nature and over-the-top extravagance. At the beginning of the movie, she's wearing Christian Dior-inspired prison stripes, her manacles are Chanel jewelry, her prison number is embroidered in glittering jet.

Costume design is not just designing pretty frocks. Each character that I work on has to have a past, even a character as extreme and as removed from reality as Cruella DeVil. It's impossible for me to design for the actor unless I know what the roots of the person being portrayed are. What are the roots of that person? Where does he come from? There has to be some basis in reality; Cruella had parents, and she grew up in a house. (For me, she came from a strictly disciplined British-in-India military family, her father a general). I prefer to think in terms of "clothes" rather than "costumes," and each outfit should tell a story and fill in another part of the jigsaw.

The Cruella we love to hate is finally revealed to the world at an outrageous fur fashion show. She wears a floor-length black suit with a tight skirt split up the front, the whole ensemble as a dragon motif. It's got dragon shoulders and an embroidered dragon that snakes all the way down the back from the shoulder blades to the ends of the train. When you first see her, she wears a half mask, which covers her eyes, and an elaborate hat with bird of paradise feathers, a huge dragon muff and custom-made dragon jewelry. There was something about seeing pink hands that was too human, so Cruella is never without gloves. Even in bed she wears gloves with her trademark fingernails, long talons, attached to the outside of the gloves. This suit was one of the last things made by the late Barbara Matera in New York, one of the world's great costume makers who made all of Glenn Close's outfits for the films, all masterpieces of the interpreter's art.

· FILMOGRAPHY ·

THE ROYAL HUNT OF THE SUN (1969) · JOE EGG (1969) · NICHOLAS AND ALEXANDRA (1971)
TRAVELS WITH MY AUNT (1972) [A.A. WINNER] · PAPILLON (1973) · THAT LUCKY TOUCH (1975)
BUFFALO BILL AND THE INDIANS (1976) · SORCERER (1977) · DEATH ON THE NILE (1978) [A.A. WINNER]
TESS (1979) [A.A. WINNER] · PRIEST OF LOVE (1981) · EVIL UNDER THE SUN (1982)
INDIANA JONES AND THE TEMPLE OF DOOM (1984) · PIRATES (1986) [A.A. NOMINATION] · ISHTAR (1987)
FRANTIC (1988) · INDIAN JONES AND THE LAST CRUSADE (1989) · HOOK (1991) [A.A. NOMINATION]
101 DALMATIANS (1996) · THE AVENGERS (1998) · THE NINTH GATE (1999)
102 DALMATIANS (2000) [A.A. NOMINATION]

Black, gold and red dragon gown of wool and silk. Decorated with metallic embroidery and multi-fabric appliqués. Designed for Glenn Close as Cruella de Vil in 102 DALMATIANS (2000).

85

SANDY POWELL

GANGS OF NEW YORK is set in a small part of New York called the Five Points, primarily between 1860 and 1863, with a flashback to 1843. Even though this world and the gangs in it actually existed, no one knew exactly how they looked. There were written descriptions, but director Martin Scorsese wanted to create our own world within this real world of America in the 1860s. I was free to stylize and to make things up, obviously based on historical accuracy, and guided by his vision. Daniel Day Lewis as Bill the Butcher is the leader of the gang the Native Americans; the 'villain' of the piece. Marty wanted him to be dandified like 1930s (or indeed even present day) gangsters who were rather vulgar about showing off their wealth. There's something more tasteful about Bill the Butcher, but I don't know whether that has to do with the character or whether it's to do with the fact that I was dressing Daniel Day Lewis.

Daniel thought he'd be a lot grubbier, a lot dirtier, not caring about his appearance. He wasn't convinced until my very first fitting with him, when we'd made prototypes of varying shapes of jacket, trousers, sleeves etc. The minute he put those things on, he said he could see the character. I didn't think it would be a battle to swing him around; when we got the clothes on him with the narrow silhouette and the original period shapes, it just came together. It was actually a good process. I just exaggerated everything about him, the whole line was lengthened, his pants were very narrow, accentuated by stripes or checks, and his boots were elongated. Daniel's hats were slightly taller than anybody else's because he could carry it off. Luckily Marty loves hats (not many directors do!) as I feel they set the tone for the whole movie.

· FILMOGRAPHY ·

CARAVAGGIO (1986) · ARIA (1987) · THE LAST OF ENGLAND (1988) · FOR QUEEN AND COUNTRY (1988)
STORMY MONDAY (1988) · VENUS PETER (1989) · KILLING DAD (1989) · THE MIRACLE (1991)
THE POPE MUST DIE (1991) · EDWARD II (1991) · THE CRYING GAME (1992)
ORLANDO (1993) [A.A. NOMINATION] · WITTGENSTEIN (1993) · BEING HUMAN (1993)
INTERVIEW WITH THE VAMPIRE (1994) · ROB ROY (1995) · MICHAEL COLLINS (1996)
THE BUTCHER BOY (1997) · THE WINGS OF THE DOVE (1997) [A.A. NOMINATION]
VELVET GOLDMINE (1998) [A.A. NOMINATION] · HILARY AND JACKIE (1998)
SHAKESPEARE IN LOVE (1998) [A.A. WINNER] · FELICIA'S JOURNEY (1999) · MISS JULIE (1999)
THE END OF THE AFFAIR (1999) · FAR FROM HEAVEN (2002)
GANGS OF NEW YORK (2002) [A.A. NOMINATION] · SYLVIA (2003) · THE AVIATOR (2004)

1840s red wool frock coat and burgundy silk vest with fireworks pattern. Narrow trousers in red and ivory plaid cotton. White linen shirt with olive green silk cravat. Designed for Daniel Day-Lewis as William 'Bill the Butcher' Cutting in GANGS OF NEW YORK (2002).

CAROL RAMSEY

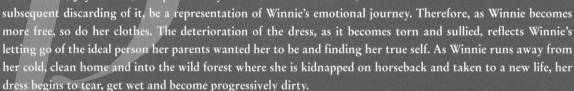

Based on the award-winning book by Natalie Babbitt, TUCK EVERLASTING is the story of Winnie Foster, a rebellious, stifled young girl who lives with her proper, uptight parents who insist on perfection. Played by Alexis Bledel, Winnie learns to embrace a new life when she discovers the answer to the ultimate cosmic question: "If you could live forever, would you?" With the story set in 1914 in a small, rural town, I wanted Winnie's immaculate dress to reflect her repressive upbringing – a pristine white dress with pink sash, black stockings and black lace-up boots. Included in the costume is an "S-Shaped" Edwardian corset to underscore the rigidity of Winnie's life.

The evolution of Winnie's emotional growth is symbolized by the loosening-up and flexibility of this integral costume, which was worn for 60% of the film. The director, Jay Russell, was particularly adamant that the corset, and the subsequent discarding of it, be a representation of Winnie's emotional journey. Therefore, as Winnie becomes more free, so do her clothes. The deterioration of the dress, as it becomes torn and sullied, reflects Winnie's letting go of the ideal person her parents wanted her to be and finding her true self. As Winnie runs away from her cold, clean home and into the wild forest where she is kidnapped on horseback and taken to a new life, her dress begins to tear, get wet and become progressively dirty.

Inspired by photographs, illustrations, fabrics, and trims of the period, the design of Winnie's costume had to satisfy period authenticity, story plot-points, color considerations, and technical stamina. I settled on three stages of aging: one clean dress and two stages of dirty.

With ager-dyer Marliss Jensen, I first made color reference charts of fabric stained with local grass, clover, dandelion leaf and flower, and Maryland mud. Marliss then made charts of paint samples to duplicate these colors. After that came a long process of breaking down the fibers, using Milsoft fabric softener and Turpenoid Natural paint solvent, painting dirt into the #2 & #3 stage dresses with Deka, Createx, and Liquitex paint, cutting and sanding rips, heat-setting the dresses, and final finesse painting. Colors used were burnt umber, yellow oxide, chromium yellow oxide green, and black.

1911 ivory cotton eyelet dress with scalloped borders and a
dusty pink silk taffeta sash. Three different versions of this
dress were made to show three stages of distressing/aging.
Designed for Alexis Bledel as Winnifred 'Winnie' Foster
in TUCK EVERLASTING (2002).

89

BOB RINGWOOD

Gore Verbinski, the director of THE TIME MACHINE, rang me up in an absolute panic, because they had already started shooting. The Victorian part of the film had been designed but none of the fantasy sequences had, and they needed costumes in two days. I told them nicely they would have to shut down for a week, which was unbelievable pressure. Luckily, I didn't even have to show them any designs. I just talked to them once and designed it. In a way, it was a very strange experience because I was given massive freedom and could do anything I fancied, as they didn't want to interfere. They just wanted something immediately. Yet I had no time to design it and very little money to spend. Jeremy Irons' warrior costume is very loosely based on samurai armor. It's really pseudo-Native American/Samurai rubber armor, I suppose.

The costume had to reveal a lot of flesh because Jeremy's scar is down his spinal column and his brain is suspended somewhere on the back of the neck. It was a backless costume, which covered his chest – really weird and very intricate. Los Angeles is so amazing because every corner has an auto shop, so I thought we'd make the armor out of car mats. We got an infinite variety of rubber car mats with patterns, curves and shapes that fit different cars. You'd be amazed. Until someone says "it's car mats" you have no idea it's car mats! I don't know how Jeremy stood up under the weight – but it wasn't unwearably heavy. The boots were made of car mats too, which was not easy and took a long time to produce. We shot for the first week without showing him below the knee, because he had no shoes. It was hysterical. All the decoration on the skirts and armor were industrial nuts and bolts, which we bashed around a bit to make them look old. Of course, when the movie is cut together it's rare that you see him from the shoulders down anyway. The poor patient man had prosthetics all over his back, a terrible wig, glass contact lenses covering his eyes, white make-up and this heavy car mat costume.

90

· FILMOGRAPHY ·

EXCALIBUR (1981) · DUNE (1984) · SANTA CLAUS (1985) · SOLARBABIES (1986)
PRICK UP YOUR EARS (1987) · EMPIRE OF THE SUN (1987) [A.A. NOMINATION] · BATMAN (1989)
CHICAGO JOE AND THE SHOWGIRL (1990) · AMERICAN FRIENDS (1991) · FROM TIME TO TIME (1992)
ALIEN 3 (1992) · BATMAN RETURNS (1992) · DEMOLITION MAN (1993) · THE SHADOW (1994)
BATMAN FOREVER (1995) · ALIEN: RESURRECTION (1997) · SUPERNOVA (2000)
A.I. ARTIFICIAL INTELLIGENCE (2001) · THE TIME MACHINE (2002)
STAR TREK: NEMESIS (2002) · TROY (2004)

Samurai armor made of rubber car mats. Skirts and armor
decorated with distressed industrial nuts and bolts.
Designed for Jeremy Irons as Uber-Morlock
in THE TIME MACHINE (2002).

PENNY ROSE

Like many actors, Johnny Depp doesn't want to talk to you when he's in the middle of another movie. For PIRATES OF THE CARRIBEAN: THE CURSE OF THE BLACK PEARL, when Johnny finally came into Cosprops in London for his first costume fitting, my associate designer John and I had obviously already discussed this pirate. We wanted the character of Jack Sparrow to be a bit of a rogue, slightly hopeless, and very thread-bare so that everything he attempts goes wrong for him. When Johnny and I were introduced I said, "What do you think of Jack Sparrow?" and he just looked me in the eye and said, "He's a rock-n-roller." During the making of the film I was probably one of the few people who knew that Jack Sparrow was based on Keith Richards. The director, Gore Verbinski, wanted the movie to look real, and in the course of my interview, while looking at paintings in my research books, he said, "Shouldn't they [the pirates] smell?" And I said, "Well, that's makeup! I just do the clothes, but yes." Gritty-real is where we were going.

Johnny tried on maybe two or three frock coats, a couple of vests and some breeches and within about half an hour Jack Sparrow was born. I had six pirate hats made in Rome and they were lying on the floor of the fitting room. But as far as Johnny was concerned, there was only one hat on that floor that was his hat, so we had twelve subsequently produced. In this first fitting, his famous knee high boots were two sizes too big for him and fur lined. I said to him, "Look, I know you love these, but they're not your size and you can't possibly have fur lined boots in the Caribbean." He said, "Oh, but I love them!" And I said, "Well, you've got to trust me about this, these boots were made by Pompeii in Rome, you will have the identical boot without the fur lining in your correct size." A week later, I met him in Paris. He paraded up and down a five star hotel in these new boots and just looked at me said, "You're good at this, aren't you?"

· FILMOGRAPHY ·

WHOSE CHILD AM I? (1974) · QUEST FOR FIRE (1981) · PINK FLOYD THE WALL (1982)
LOCAL HERO (1983) · ANOTHER COUNTRY (1984) · CAL (1984) · THE COMMITMENTS (1991)
UNDER SUSPICION (1991) · MAP OF THE HUMAN HEART (1993) · SPLITTING HEIRS (1993)
SHADOWLANDS (1993) · THE ROAD TO WELLVILLE (1994) · CARRINGTON (1995)
MISSION: IMPOSSIBLE (1996) · EVITA (1996) · IN LOVE AND WAR (1996) · THE PARENT TRAP (1998)
ENTRAPMENT (1999) · JUST VISITING (2001) · THE GOOD THIEF (2002) · THE SLEEPING DICTIONARY (2003)
PIRATES OF THE CARIBBEAN: THE CURSE OF THE BLACK PEARL (2003)
KING ARTHUR (2004) · THE WEATHER MAN (2004)

Late 17th-century black linen-weave frock coat and gray waistcoat with silver buttons. Ivory linen shirt, worn black breeches and pirate boots. Designed for Johnny Depp as Jack Sparrow in PIRATES OF THE CARIBBEAN: THE CURSE OF THE BLACK PEARL (2003).

ANN ROTH

When the actor comes into the fitting room for the first fitting, he or she is at a disadvantage. I can't pretend that the muslin or mock-up that I've started is a collaboration between the actor and me. I had been thinking about it for some time – planning the shape, fabric, balance, trimming. Often I like the make-up/hair designer to be present, and then, along with the costume maker, the creation starts its birth. The actor slowly becomes a character.

Ada Monroe, played by the great actress Nicole Kidman in COLD MOUNTAIN, is a Charleston girl, raised in gentility. When her father's health causes them to move to the very high, rough elevations of western North Carolina's "Cold Mountain," she travels with her trunk of southern lady finery. Her father dies there, the Civil War takes its toll, and she is left pretty much to survive on their small farm without any practical knowledge.

Her clothes deteriorate and, for instance, a beautifully quilted taffeta petticoat, originally worn over the hoop skirt to soften the effect of bones, now becomes a warm skirt worn over a manure-spattered pair of her father's trousers. His one fine coat becomes her warm covering. She loses weight and her clothes are torn and stained. She makes a scarecrow out of the dress she wore when she kissed her beau, Inman, goodbye as he goes off to war.

· FILMOGRAPHY ·

THE WORLD OF HENRY ORIENT (1964) · UP THE DOWN STAIRCASE (1967) · MIDNIGHT COWBOY (1969)
KLUTE (1971) · THE DAY OF THE LOCUST (1975) · MURDER BY DEATH (1976) · THE GOODBYE GIRL (1977)
COMING HOME (1978) · CALIFORNIA SUITE (1978) · HAIR (1979) · DRESSED TO KILL (1980)
NINE TO FIVE (1980) · ONLY WHEN I LAUGH (1981) · THE WORLD ACCORDING TO GARP (1982)
SILKWOOD (1983) · PLACES IN THE HEART (1984) [A.A. NOMINATION] · THE SLUGGER'S WIFE (1985)
JAGGED EDGE (1985) · SWEET DREAMS (1985) · HEARTBURN (1986) · THE MORNING AFTER (1986)
THE UNBEARABLE LIGHTNESS OF BEING (1988) · BILOXI BLUES (1988) · WORKING GIRL (1988) · HER ALIBI (1989)
POSTCARDS FROM THE EDGE (1990) · PACIFIC HEIGHTS (1990) · THE BONFIRE OF THE VANITIES (1990)
REGARDING HENRY (1991) · THE MAMBO KINGS (1992) · A STRANGER AMONG US (1992) · SCHOOL TIES (1992)
DAVE (1993) · DENNIS THE MENACE (1993) · GUARDING TESS (1994) · WOLF (1994) · SABRINA (1995)
THE BIRDCAGE (1996) · THE ENGLISH PATIENT (1996) [A.A. WINNER] · IN & OUT (1997)
PRIMARY COLORS (1998) · THE SIEGE (1998) · THE OUT-OF-TOWNERS (1999)
THE TALENTED MR. RIPLEY (1999) [A.A. NOMINATION WITH GARY JONES] · FINDING FORRESTER (2000)
SOMEONE LIKE YOU (2001) · CHANGING LANES (2002) · SIGNS (2002) · ADAPTATION (2002)
THE HOURS (2002) [A.A. NOMINATION] · COLD MOUNTAIN (2003) · THE STEPFORD WIVES (2004) · THE VILLAGE (2004)

94

1860s silk burgundy bodice, sage green quilted
silk petticoat. Copper and green diamond
patterned long skirt and black wool trousers.
Designed for Nicole Kidman as Ada Monroe
in COLD MOUNTAIN (2003).

MAY ROUTH

In Paris on a September day in 1997, John Frankenheimer presided over a great lunch to outline his vision of RONIN. Also present were production designer Michael Hanan and cinematographer Robert Fraisse. John was inspired by the gritty realism of director Gillo Pontecorvo's 1965 classic THE BATTLE OF ALGIERS. This was the fourth consecutive year working with John, and by now I had learned his likes and dislikes. I understood that fierce colors were abhorrent to him, preferring to have the actors in understated costumes.

RONIN was a highly intelligent thriller, and most of our principals, led by Robert De Niro, played members of an international criminal gang, professional killers. This group of hired guns cross, double cross and triple cross one another during the course of the film. My challenge was to dress them to reflect their individual characters, but with an overall degree of anonymity. The film was ultimately filmed in Paris and the South of France. In one sequence, shot in an exclusive hotel, De Niro and Natascha McElhone had to blend in with the sophisticated clientele, which necessitated a distinct change of appearance. I shopped in Monte Carlo for Robert, where I found a great brown suede jacket. In combination with a gray cashmere sweater he looked very elegant. Natasha looked beautiful in a Pierre Cardin jacket and pants, rather than a skirt, which gave her a distinct edge.

John was one of the few directors who recognized and acknowledged the important contribution of a costume designer to any production.... I miss him.

· FILMOGRAPHY ·
THE MAN WHO FELL TO EARTH (1976) · THE LAST REMAKE OF BEAU GESTE (1977)
SGT. PEPPER'S LONELY HEARTS CLUB BAND (1978) · BEING THERE (1979) · FIRST FAMILY (1980)
GHOST STORY (1981) · MY FAVORITE YEAR (1982) · SPLASH (1984)
NEWSIES (1992) · RONIN (1998) · REINDEER GAMES (2000) · THE HIRE: AMBUSH (2001)

Black leather jacket with beige, red and black plaid lining. Button-down shirt of oversized plaid in dark gray and beige. Blue denim jeans. Designed for Robert De Niro as Sam in RONIN (1998).

RITA
RYACK

I still believe, with two attempts at Dr. Seuss in my canon, that it's not possible to reproduce the animation and energy of his line drawing into three dimensions – not to mention that those "Whos down in Whoville" wear only the most abbreviated suggestion of clothing. We tried to develop our own visual vocabulary for the world of Whoville, and to make preparation for their Christmas Whobilation, the most important part of their culture.

I used references from the late 1950s, when Dr. Seuss' "How the Grinch Stole Christmas" was published, for period ambience and ideas for holiday crafts. The ultimate Christmas offering is the fruitcake. I created quite a few specialty costumes based on Christmas food: a popcorn ball, a Swedish tea-ring hat, hats of eggnog cups and bowls, and crocheted capelets festooned with cookies and sugared jellied candy slices. I used reds and greens as neutrals for the background Whos, who wore simple graphic sweaters knit to accommodate their pear-shaped, padded bodies. The "Fruitcake Fellow's" hat was a glob of whipped cream with a cherry on top.

· FILMOGRAPHY ·
AFTER HOURS (1985) · SUSPECT (1987) · THE HOUSE ON CARROLL STREET (1988)
CROSSING DELANCEY (1988) · PENN & TELLER GET KILLED (1989) · AN INNOCENT MAN (1989)
CLASS ACTION (1991) · CAPE FEAR (1991) · MAD DOG AND GLORY (1993) · A BRONX TALE (1993)
MR. JONES (1994) · THE PAPER (1994) · APOLLO 13 (1995) · CASINO (1995) · THE FAN (1996)
RANSOM (1996) · WAG THE DOG (1997) · MY GIANT (1998) · EDTV (1999)
BRINGING OUT THE DEAD (1999) · HOW THE GRINCH STOLE CHRISTMAS (2000) [A.A. NOMINATION]
RUSH HOUR 2 (2001) · A BEAUTIFUL MIND (2001) · THE HUMAN STAIN (2003)
THE CAT IN THE HAT (2003) · AFTER THE SUNSET (2004)

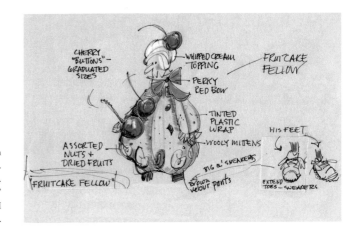

Multi-color fruitcake costume made of L-200 foam
covered in vinyl. Brown cotton velour trousers.
Whipped cream and cherry hat.
Designed for Christmas Fruitcake "Who"
in DR. SEUSS' HOW THE GRINCH
STOLE CHRISTMAS (2000).

MARIA SCHICKER

The EXTREME OPS story was premised on a film crew shooting a commercial for "the ultimate video camera" used by the extreme sports crowd. Christian Duguay, the film's director, wanted a fun, colorful, and futuristic look for the film. He needed bright colors to help spot the actors in water and snow. The costumes not only had to serve the demands of the story; they also needed to keep the actors warm, dry, and attractive.

My research brought me together with mountaineers, professional skiers, kayakers, skydivers and stunt people. They all had their favorite outfits and materials, depending on seasonal conditions, and I learned a lot about the complexity of the needs of extreme sports garments. The cinematographer and I also did screen tests in snow, ice and water, with different film stock as well as different filters and exposures. My intense research of international fabric sources led me to a factory in Denmark that provided me with the high-tech fabrics I needed.

Each of the characters, good or bad, had their own look, style, and creative approach. We needed at least ten copies of each costume, prepped for different aging stages, for the actors and their stunt doubles. I also had to make sure that everything I designed kept the actors warm in subzero weather. For the commercial scenes, I designed costumes that were loud, borderline kitsch, innocent and as dare-devilish as seemed appropriate. The film was about speed. I hadn't yet worked on costumes whose prime mission was to go as fast as possible. I decided to highlight all sports costumes with 3M reflective tape. The material played well in all lighting conditions, adding to the sense of speed. In addition, it actually helped to make the actors look thinner. An Austrian ski garment company loved the idea, and used my designs for their collection last season.

· FILMOGRAPHY ·
DER WESTEN LEUCHTET (1982) · SUPER (1984) · KAMINSKY- EIN BULLE DREHT DURCH (1985)
ZISCHKE (1986) · THE JOURNEY (1986) · EIN SCHWEIZER NAMENS N`TZLI (1988)
DER DOPPELTE N`TZLI (1990) · ALL LIES (1992) · THE QUALITY OF MERCY (1994)
AN AMERICAN WEREWOLF IN PARIS (1997) · DEBT OF LOVE (1997) · MARLENE (2000)
TO PROTECT AND SERVE (2001) · THE 51ST STATE (2001) · EXTREME OPS (2002)

MARIA SCHICKER
COSTUME DESIGNER

Bridgette Wilson-Sampras
as
CHLOE
'THE COMMERCIAL COSTUME'

Fluorescent pink ski jacket of water resistant nylon
lined with gray fleece cotton. Polypropylene
shirt and wool sweater. Black nylon trousers.
Designed for Bridgette Wilson-Sampras
as Chloe in EXTREME OPS (2002).

LAURA JEAN SHANNON

The first time I met Will Ferrell, he and director Jon Favreau were in a writing session. I said, "I'm gonna put you in tights for the next six months. Are you still gonna talk to me at the end of it?" Will's response was, "Hey, no problem!" He was always absolutely good for the game. Jon's vision was for ELF to appeal to all audiences, not just children. He wanted to evoke a feeling of our childhood. What we wanted was to create an elf costume that was a realistic version of all of the elves you see in the TV Christmas specials. We were working backwards by taking the iconic imagery of all elves and incorporating those elements into a fully functional costume. I created very specific rules about what was allowed in the North Pole. We wanted the elves to be people of the world with roots in various cultures. Their world was very low-tech, and their clothes and tools were all things that they could find in the North Pole. The fabric with which we built Will's and the elves' costumes needed to be practical for surviving in the North Pole. I wanted to make the costumes out of boiled wool since the North Pole is such a chilly place. Besides being awfully hot, on camera it lacked the textural quality we were looking for. We went with a lighter weight cream color bouclé wool that we dyed a rich grassy green, starting with that fabulous texture; after we dyed it, it had even more textural quality that translated well onto film.

Jon and I wanted a major juxtaposition between Will's elf costume and the elf costumes of the sad "rent-an-elves" at Gimble's. We wanted Will to stand out – like a real class act, a real elf. I was vehement about not wanting zippers on the elves. I hated the idea of having these fabulously constructed costumes, and for convenience sake, risking the possibility of the glare of Will's zipper catching the light. We had some pretty interesting fittings. Will wore a cut-away jacket and tights while running around the streets of Manhattan   for many scenes; he tried on every imaginable undergarment and worked out all the kinks, he always had the best attitude. Will brought the costume to life, and considering he was the one wearing tights every day, he was a good sport.

· FILMOGRAPHY ·
DROP DEAD ROCK (1995) · THE LAST HOME RUN (1996) · JADED (1996)
NIAGARA, NIAGARA (1997) · CLAIRE DOLAN (1998) · REQUIEM FOR A DREAM (2000)
PRINCE OF CENTRAL PARK (2000) · THE SAFETY OF OBJECTS (2001) · MADE (2001)
I'M WITH LUCY (2002) · ANYTHING ELSE (2003) · ELF (2003) · BLADE: TRINITY (2004)

Hand-dyed boucle wool dovetail jacket lined with dark green cotton sateen,
with metallic gold and green embroidery, bunny fur collar and cuffs.
Coordinating elf hat. Gold polar fleece tights, black leather elf shoes.
Designed for Will Ferrell as Buddy in ELF (2003).

103

JULIE WEISS

Frida Kahlo was an extraordinary woman, an artist who left a visual recording of her life. Through her paintings Frida was viewed, not only as the world saw her, but as she saw herself, spilling forth onto her canvas of color and memory. Frida embraced her Mexican heritage, wearing traditional clothing while living a non-traditional life. When she walked down the street, she exuded an aura. She didn't demand "look at me," but rather, "this is who I am."

As costume designers, we often help create fictional characters through their dress, defining life's choices. But Frida's life existed in such a powerful way that she still exists. Her art is part of Mexico's heritage, shared by all who choose to see. Frida's life was short & intense (1907-1954). Her portraits show her extreme physical pain, mental anguish and acute political awareness. Dressing Salma Hayek was dressing Frida Kahlo. At the moment the camera rolled, the two women had merged and the costume had turned to clothing.

The Story of the Green Dress: When Frida was to marry Diego Rivera, she wore a traditional wedding gown, Victorian style with European lace and a silk veil with a coronet of corn flowers. However, it was the dress of Frida's attendant, Aurora, that held Frida's spirit. Hers was a traditional Tehuana gown of lush green worn with a red silk rebozo, Oaxacan gold jewelry, green beads and petticoats made from everyday cotton prints: a true combination. It was Aurora's pride of her people, her roots, that Frida was drawn to. And so the exchange began. Frida left behind the white dress of obedience and donned a dress of even greater stature and royalty. This was the Frida Kahlo that Diego Rivera married.

· FILMOGRAPHY ·

TESTAMENT (1983) · SECOND THOUGHTS (1983) · F/X (1986) · THE WHALES OF AUGUST (1987)
CHERRY 2000 (1987) · TEQUILA SUNRISE (1988) · STEEL MAGNOLIAS (1989) · THE FRESHMAN (1990)
HONEYMOON IN VEGAS (1992) · SEARCHING FOR BOBBY FISCHER (1993) · NAKED IN NEW YORK (1993)
IT COULD HAPPEN TO YOU (1994) · 12 MONKEYS (1995) [A.A. NOMINATION] · MARVIN'S ROOM (1996)
TOUCH (1997) · THE EDGE (1997) · FEAR AND LOATHING IN LAS VEGAS (1998) · A SIMPLE PLAN (1998)
AMERICAN BEAUTY (1999) · ISN'T SHE GREAT (2000) · GET CARTER (2000) · THE GIFT (2000)
HEARTS IN ATLANTIS (2001) · FRIDA (2002) [A.A. NOMINATION] · AUTO FOCUS (2002)
THE RING (2002) · THE MISSING (2003)

Early 20th-century ensemble of silk damask, with embroidery.
Calico slips and corset of silk faille and white batiste.
Designed for Salma Hayek as Frida Kahlo in FRIDA (2002).

JACQUELINE WEST

The idea for this unique period costume originated from Doug Wright's beautiful script for QUILLS. Philip Kaufman, the director, wanted the Marquis de Sade, played by Geoffrey Rush, in one costume for his entire time in prison, as he supposedly lived in one suit for 25 years. Phillip envisioned a pristine white peau de soie suit declining into tatters – a fabulous 1790's suit turning into rags. In prison, all of the Marquis de Sade's writing implements were confiscated – he had no paper, and no ink. He resorts to writing in his own blood upon the only object left to write on – his suit. A script note said that he broke a glass in his cell, cut his finger and spent the whole night writing until he was too weak to write from the loss of blood. (He would dip the glass shard into his blood and write). There is only one suit written in blood, because it was so expensive and labor intensive for us to produce. It took six weeks for Cosprops in London to make, supervised by Suzi Turnbull. We hand stitched the original suit, shredded and aged it to a parchment color, and then it was taken apart and silk-screened as flat pieces.

Francis Bennett wonderfully mastered the Marquis de Sade's handwriting from an original manuscript. For blood, we experimented with cow's blood but it dried black. So we ended up using a mixture of thinned cow's blood and red tempera paint. Jane Clive, the ager, first practiced writing lines on a shirtsleeve toile from Cosprops. Jane would dip a quill in the mixture of blood, and where the quill would run out of blood, the lettering would lighten, just as it would on paper. The writing would get smaller where the Marquis would have tried to cram in words before coming to a seam. To speed the process, Jane made silkscreen plates from the pattern pieces; but there were places where we were unable to silkscreen, and these were filled in by hand. The silk screens themselves took almost four days for each pattern piece. We would sit with a glass of wine for nine hours, repeated over many weeks, recreating the mad writing with Jane forging the Marquis' handwriting, while writing the story of Ganymede on his suit. It was beautiful to watch.

· FILMOGRAPHY ·
RISING SUN (1993) · QUILLS (2000) [A.A. NOMINATION] · JUST ONE NIGHT (2000) · THE BANGER SISTERS (2002)
LEO (2002) · THE LEAGUE OF EXTRAORDINARY GENTLEMEN (2003) · DOWN IN THE VALLEY (2004)

Late 18th-century silk Peau de Soie aristocratic man's suit
in ecru with red writing in tempura and cows blood.
Ecru coat and britches with silver waistcoat.
Designed for Geoffrey Rush as The Marquis de Sade
in QUILLS (2000).

107

ALBERT WOLSKY

ROAD TO PERDITION is set mostly outdoors in and out of Chicago during the winter of 1932-1933. After extensive research, I began my design process trying original period garments on Tom Hanks to see how they fall and move. It's the way I usually start. Dan Striepeke, the make-up artist, also wanted to experiment with a mustache and a slight nose bridge. Our director, Sam Mendes, was in Chicago and we were in Los Angeles. To show him the direction and shape we were taking, we decided to dress Hanks in period clothes and make-up and photograph him in Super 8 and still photos and send them to Mendes. It was like doing our own screen test. It helped us a great deal for it showed Mendes our image and gave me a direction for Hanks' character. Sullivan, his character, is basically in one costume running away with his son. Being bitter winter, the most important costume was his coat, long and enveloping. I also knew I wanted the entire film to be dark and without color.

Arriving at this image was the simple part. Realizing it was close to a nightmare. You can't realize a period without the right fabrics. This particular Depression period had thick and heavy coarse fabrics. Fabrics totally unavailable today. After a first fitting, I realized I was in trouble. Nothing looked or fell right or moved the way it should. Out of total desperation, my assistants Marcy Froehlich and Susan Hall mentioned a weaver they both knew. Reluctantly, feeling that it was never going to work, we sent her a period suit to see if she could replicate the fabric. Rabbit Goody, and that is her name, did it brilliantly. Thus began a wonderful collaboration. Samples would go back and forth cross-country until we could arrive at the right weight, weave and color. I was able to get exactly what was needed both for the character and period. I could never have gotten the silhouette and movement with existing fabric. Everything that Tom Hanks wore was woven for him. We even managed to weave fabric for Jude Law and a few other characters. This was the single most important contribution to achieving the total look I was searching for.

· FILMOGRAPHY ·

THE HEART IS A LONELY HUNTER (1968) · LOVING (1970) · LOVERS AND OTHER STRANGERS (1970)
UP THE SANDBOX (1972) · HARRY AND TONTO (1974) · LENNY (1974) · THE TURNING POINT (1977)
AN UNMARRIED WOMAN (1978) · GREASE (1978) · MANHATTAN (1979)
ALL THAT JAZZ (1979) [A.A. WINNER] · THE JAZZ SINGER (1980) · ALL NIGHT LONG (1981) · TEMPEST (1982)
STILL OF THE NIGHT (1982) · SOPHIE'S CHOICE (1982) [A.A. NOMINATION] · STAR 80 (1983)
MOSCOW ON THE HUDSON (1984) · THE FALCON AND THE SNOWMAN (1985)
THE JOURNEY OF NATTY GANN (1985) [A.A. NOMINATION] · DOWN AND OUT IN BEVERLY HILLS (1986)
LEGAL EAGLES (1986) · CRIMES OF THE HEART (1986) · NADINE (1987) · MOON OVER PARADOR (1988)
CHANCES ARE (1989) · ENEMIES: A LOVE STORY (1989) · FUNNY ABOUT LOVE (1990) · SCENES FROM A MALL (1991)
BUGSY (1991) [A.A. WINNER] · TOYS (1992) [A.A. NOMINATION] · FATAL INSTINCT (1993) · THE PELICAN BRIEF (1993)
JUNIOR (1994) · THE GRASS HARP (1995) · UP CLOSE & PERSONAL (1996) · STRIPTEASE (1996) · THE JACKAL (1997)
YOU'VE GOT MAIL (1998) · RUNAWAY BRIDE (1999) · GALAXY QUEST (1999) · LUCKY NUMBERS (2000)
ROAD TO PERDITION (2002) · MAID IN MANHATTAN (2002) · THE MANCHURIAN CANDIDATE (2004)

1931 black hand-woven wool overcoat. Button-down
cotton shirt, rayon tie and gray fedora.
Designed for Tom Hanks as Michael 'Mike' Sullivan
in ROAD TO PERDITION (2002).

109

DURINDA WOOD

I believe that comedy comes from reality. The Marx Brothers and Monty Python movies wouldn't be as funny if the whole background of the film wasn't entirely real. A MIGHTY WIND is supposed to be a documentary and the director, Christopher Guest, and I really cared about recreating and being truthful to the folk music era. Chris talks with his familiar ensemble of actors first and they work out who each character is: where the person is from, what their history is, and what their motivations are. We really all collaborate on creating specific characters while embracing all of the humorous oddities of real life. They'll tell me what they're going to be doing during the scenes, but sometimes they don't know because so much depends on the improvisation at that moment when the camera starts filming. That's what you'll experience in all of Chris's films.

First, the entire company will get a script that isn't a script – it's just an outline of action. It's all improvised and the crew doesn't know what's going to happen until the actors start saying the words. So all of us have to be extremely flexible with Chris's filmmaking style. The actors start to discover their characters through their wigs, their hair and the look of their face, continuing down to their costume. Judi Cooper-Sealy, the hairdresser from Second City, has been working with Eugene Levy and Catherine O'Hara for twenty years. For Chris's films I create a large closet full of accessories and costumes for each character, as designers commonly do for an episodic television show, and then I'm able to make instant changes on the set if I need to. We definitely have fittings before shooting and try to work out in advance every possibility for each scene in those fittings. A MIGHTY WIND is about three famous folk groups of the sixties, the Folksmen, Mitch and Mickey and the Main Street Singers. Sissy Knox (Parker Posey) was one of the newer members of the "new" Main Street Singers, replacing her father who was one of the original members. They prided themselves on the zesty and colorful energy that they brought to folk. For research, I watched folk concerts and documentaries about folk music, beatniks, and the Newport Festival. We had all the period research plastered on the walls of the production office and everyone was trying to top each other by finding the craziest looking '60s album cover.

· FILMOGRAPHY ·
BATTLE BEYOND THE STARS (1980) · MARIA'S LOVERS (1984) · THE SURE THING (1985)
BACK TO SCHOOL (1986) · THE SEVENTH SIGN (1988) · A TIME OF DESTINY (1988)
ANIMAL BEHAVIOR (1989) · SIBLING RIVALRY (1990) · THE VANISHING (1993)
THE BEATNIKS (1993) ALMOST HEROES (1998) · PROS AND CONS (1999 · BEST IN SHOW (2000)
MULHOLLAND DRIVE (2001) · A MIGHTY WIND (2003)

Cotton jersey/rayon yellow short sleeve shirt.
Royal blue and turquoise pleated skirt.
Designed for Parker Posey as Sissy Knox in
A MIGHTY WIND (2003).

JANTY YATES

Ridley Scott described his vision of GLADIATOR during two or three hours at my first meeting with him, and I left both moved and inspired. It was imperative to Ridley that Russell Crowe look manly and virile despite the required Roman tunic. I was after the ragged look of a Scotsman in his kilt. For research I used books, paintings, the British Museum, the internet, libraries and all of Rome, Pompeii, Herculaneum, but definitively avoided period films. We created mood boards plus a traveling library of 25-30 relevant files of research. Each character was delineated very clearly so that their costume story was simple and clear. Russell went from general to slave, to gladiator-in-training, to gladiator number one. Joaquin Phoenix was less ornate when he was emperor-in-waiting and he became more flamboyant as his madness emerged. I always work in close collaboration with actors. An unhappy actor makes for not a good performance.

The production design for Rome was inspired by the palette of the pre-Raphaelite paintings of Sir Lawrence Alma-Tadema, pastel pistachios, pinks, almonds and sky blue. We took the Roman females and made them pre-Raphaelite maidens. Throughout the sequences in Morocco the color palette was sand and sky, but when we arrived in Germania it became monochrome with rich texture and color on the principals. Color definitely helped the mood of each scene. The costume design did not stray too far from historical fact, but I took liberties with the armor. In terms of accuracy, we changed the shape of most helmets, lengthened all the tunics to knee length, and altered some breastplate shapes. All fabrics, armors and leather were very textured and very authentically aged. Fur was a specific accessory for both Russell Crowe and actress Connie Nielson. We had six months prep and we researched right up until the first day of principal photography.

· FILMOGRAPHY ·

BAD BEHAVIOR (1993) · THE ENGLISHMAN WHO WENT UP A HILL BUT CAME DOWN A MOUNTAIN (1995)
JUDE (1996) · WELCOME TO SARAJEVO (1997) · THE MAN WHO KNEW TOO LITTLE (1997)
PLUNKETT & MACLEANE (1999) · WITH OR WITHOUT YOU (1999) · GLADIATOR (2000) [A.A. WINNER]
ENEMY AT THE GATES (2001) · HANNIBAL (2001) · CHARLOTTE GRAY (2001) · DE-LOVELY (2004)

Ivory painted leather decorated breastplate and
ivory tunic. Shin guards and gauntlets.
Designed for Joaquin Phoenix as Commodus
in GLADIATOR (2000).

MARY ZOPHRES

Joel and Ethan Coen's scripts are incredibly evocative. It's not that they describe how the characters are dressed, but from their description it is clear how they should be dressed. When I read their scripts I can imagine exactly how the movie will look. During design meetings we use the costume sketches as a springboard for discussions about character. Catherine Zeta-Jones played a scheming man-eater in INTOLERABLE CRUELTY, and every costume change she wears was for a specific premeditated reason. When she went to court she dressed in a demure, soft pink dress, matching belt, shoes, handbag. When she seduces George Clooney, she's in a gold-beaded dress; when he comes to her rescue, she's in purple lingerie and when she leaves him she's in a black and white hound's-tooth suit with a giant brimmed black hat. I don't know how to say this in a proper way, but it's a very 'screw you' costume change. Catherine wears this wedding gown as part of her grand scheme to convince George that she is marrying an oil tycoon, Billy Bob Thornton. In reality, he is only a soap opera actor and the wedding is a fake.

Catherine is a dream for a costume designer to dress because she knows how to angle her body and to walk for the camera. There's one scene where Catherine has a poodle in one hand, a clutch purse in the other and wears a pair of 4 1/2 inch spike heels. She navigates herself down very steep steps at Caesar's Palace as if she werc in a pair of sneakers, but in an extremely sexy way. She agreed with the classic, sexy approach for her character and we were completely in sync. We kept her in solids and rich beautiful colors, and I did end up having to design and make quite a bit of her costumes. Catherine will sit for hours for a fitting while you're pinning things on her, and she'll have endless amounts of fittings if you need them. Catherine wants to look good and she's totally fine with taking the time to make sure that she does. I don't think I've ever worked with an actress who can work it like Catherine can. To me she's the closest thing to old Hollywood glamour that Hollywood has to offer.

· FILMOGRAPHY ·

PCU (1994) · Dumb & Dumber (1994) · Fargo (1996) · Kingpin (1996)
The Last of the High Kings (1996) · Playing God (1997) · Digging to China (1998)
Thick as Thieves (1998) · The Big Lebowski (1998) · Paulie (1998)
There's Something about Mary (1998) · Any Given Sunday (1999)
O Brother, Where Art Thou? (2000) · Ghost World (2000) · The Man Who Wasn't There (2001)
Moonlight Mile (2002) · Catch Me If You Can (2002) · View from the Top (2003)
Intolerable Cruelty (2003) · The Ladykillers (2004) · The Terminal (2004)

Ivory wedding dress of double-faced satin with fitted bodice. Full
skirt using 60 yards of nylon tulle.
Designed for Catherine Zeta-Jones as Marylin Rexroth
in INTOLERABLE CRUELTY (2003).

115

INDEX

Sketch illustrator noted if other than designer

SARA EDWARDS
UPTOWN GIRLS, MGM, 2003.
Photograph and sketch of costume designed for Brittany Murphy as Molly Gunn; p. 34

APRIL FERRY
TERMINATOR 3: RISE OF THE MACHINES, Warner Bros. Pictures, 2003. Photograph and sketch of costume designed for Arnold Schwarzenegger as Terminator; sketch illustrator: Jacqueline Wazir; p. 36

BRUCE FINLAYSON
GODS AND MONSTERS, Lions Gate Films, 1998.
Photograph and sketch of costume designed for Cornelia Hayes O'Herlihy as Princess Margaret; p. 38

MARIE FRANCE
BLACK KNIGHT, Twentieth Century Fox, 2001.
Photograph and sketch of costume designed for Martin Lawrence as Jamal Walker (aka Skywalker);
sketch illustrator: Lois DeArmond; p. 40

GLORIA GRESHAM
BANDITS, MGM; 2001.
Photograph and sketch of costume designed for Billy Bob Thornton as Terry Lee Collins;
sketch illustrator: Gina Flanagan; p. 42

BETSY HEIMANN
ALMOST FAMOUS, DreamWorks Pictures and Columbia Pictures, 2000. Photograph and sketch of costume designed for Kate Hudson as Penny Lane; p. 44

JOANNA JOHNSTON
LOVE ACTUALLY, Universal Pictures and Studio Canal, 2003. Photograph and sketch of costume designed for Keira Knightley as Juliet; sketch illustrator: Jeanne Spaziani; p. 46

GARY JONES
TWO WEEKS NOTICE, Warner Bros. Pictures, 2002.
Photograph and sketch of costume designed for Sandra Bullock as Lucy Kelson; sketch illustrator: Pablo Borges ; p. 48

RENÉE EHRLICH KALFUS
CHOCOLAT, Miramax Films, 2000.
Photograph and sketch of costume designed for Juliette Binoche as Vianne Rocher; p. 50

MICHAEL KAPLAN
FIGHT CLUB, Twentieth Century Fox, 1999.
Photograph and sketch of costume designed for Brad Pitt as Tyler Durden; sketch illustrator: Pauline Annon; p. 52

CHRISI KARVONIDES-DUSHENKO
BEAUTIFUL, Destination Films, 2000.
Photograph and sketch of costume designed for Minnie Driver as Mona Hibbard; p. 54

JEFFREY KURLAND
OCEAN'S ELEVEN, Warner Bros. Pictures, 2001.
Photograph and sketch of costume designed for Julia Roberts as Tess Ocean; p. 56

DAN LESTER
THE CORE, Paramount Pictures, 2003.
Photograph and sketch of costume designed for Delroy Lindo as Dr. Ed 'Braz' Brazzleton;
sketch illustrator: Shawna Leavell Trpcic; p. 58

117

CAROL RAMSEY
TUCK EVERLASTING, Buena Vista Pictures, 2002.
Photographs and sketch of costume designed for Alexis Bledel as Winnifred 'Winnie' Foster;
sketch illustrator: Lois DeArmond; p. 88

BOB RINGWOOD
THE TIME MACHINE, DreamWorks Pictures and Warner Bros. Pictures, 2002.
Photographs of Jeremy Irons as Uber-Morlock; p. 90

PENNY ROSE
PIRATES OF THE CARIBBEAN: THE CURSE OF THE BLACK PEARL, Buena Vista Pictures, 2003.
Photograph and sketch of costume designed for Johnny Depp as Jack Sparrow; p. 92

ANN ROTH
COLD MOUNTAIN, Miramax Films, 2003.
Photograph and sketch of costume designed for Nicole Kidman as Ada Monroe; p. 94

MAY ROUTH
RONIN, MGM, 1998. Photograph and sketch of costume designed for Robert De Niro as Sam: p. 96

RITA RYACK
DR. SEUSS' HOW THE GRINCH STOLE CHRISTMAS, Universal Pictures, 2000.
Photograph and sketch of costume designed for Christmas Fruitcake "Who;" p. 98

MARIA SCHICKER
EXTREME OPS, Paramount Pictures/MDP Worldwide/Diamant Cohen Productions, 2002.
Photograph and sketch of costume designed for Bridgette Wilson-Sampras as Chloe; p. 100

LAURA JEAN SHANNON
ELF, New Line Cinema, 2003.
Photograph and sketch of costume designed for Will Ferrell as Buddy; sketch illustrator: Jayne Mabbott; p. 102

JULIE WEISS
FRIDA, Miramax Films, 2002.
Photograph and sketch of costume designed for Salma Hayek as Frida Kahlo; p. 104

JACQUELINE WEST
QUILLS, Fox Searchlight Pictures, 2000.
Photograph and sketch of costume designed for Geoffrey Rush as The Marquis de Sade;
sketch illustrator: Carlos Rosario; p. 106

ALBERT WOLSKY
ROAD TO PERDITION, DreamWorks Pictures and Twentieth Century Fox, 2002.
Photograph and sketch of costume designed for Tom Hanks as Michael 'Mike' Sullivan; p. 108

DURINDA WOOD
A MIGHTY WIND, Warner Bros. Pictures, 2003.
Photograph and sketch of costume designed for Parker Posey as Sissy Knox; sketch illustrator: Anna Wyckoff; p. 110

JANTY YATES
GLADIATOR, DreamWorks Pictures and Universal Pictures, 2000.
Photograph and sketch of costume designed for Joaquin Phoenix as Commodus; sketch illustrator: Sammy Howarth; p. 112

MARY ZOPHRES
INTOLERABLE CRUELTY, Universal Pictures, 2003.
Photograph and sketch of costume designed for Catherine Zeta-Jones as Marylin Rexroth; p. 114

PHOTO CREDITS

Page 9:   *Spider-Man* ©2002 Columbia Pictures Industries, Inc. All Rights Reserved. Courtesy of Columbia Pictures.

Page 11:   *Austin Powers in Goldmember.* Copyright 2002, New Line Productions, Inc. All Rights Reserved. Still appears courtesy of New Line Productions, Inc.

Page 13:   *Big Fish* ©2003 Columbia Pictures Industries, Inc. All Rights Reserved. Courtesy of Columbia Pictures.

Page 15:   *The Matrix Reloaded* © 2003 WV Films III LLC. All Rights Reserved.

Page 17:   *Possession* © 2002 Warner Bros., a division of Time Warner Entertainment Company L.P. and Universal City Studios Productions LLLP. All Rights Reserved.

Page 19:   *Punch-Drunk Love* ©2002 Columbia Pictures Industries, Inc. All Rights Reserved. Courtesy of Columbia Pictures.

Page 21:   Still taken from *The Cooler* provided through the courtesy of Lions Gate Entertainment.

Page 23:   *The Affair of the Necklace* © 2001 Affair Productions, LLC. All Rights Reserved.

Page 25:   *Legally Blonde 2: Red, White & Blonde* ©2003 Metro-Goldwyn-Mayer Pictures Inc. All Rights Reserved.

Page 27:   *Shaft.* © Paramount Pictures. All Rights Reserved.

Page 29:   *What a Girl Wants* © 2003 Warner Bros. Entertainment Inc. and Gaylord Films LLC. All Rights Reserved.

Page 31:   Photograph by Francois Duhamel for the motion picture *What Lies Beneath* © 2000 DreamWorks L.L.C. and 20th Century Fox.

Page 33:   *The Last Samurai* © 2003 Warner Bros. Entertainment Inc. All Rights Reserved.

Page 35:   *Uptown Girls* ©2003 Metro-Goldwyn-Mayer Pictures Inc. All Rights Reserved.

Page 37:   *Terminator 3: Rise of the Machines* TM © 2003 IMF Internationale Medien und Film GmbH & Co. 3 Produktions KG.

Page 39:   Still taken from *Gods and Monsters* provided through the courtesy of Lions Gate Entertainment.

Page 41:   *Black Knight* ©2001 Twentieth Century Fox, Monarchy Enterprises S.a.r.l. and Regency Entertainment (USA), Inc. All Rights Reserved.

Page 43:   *Bandits* ©2001 Metro-Goldwyn-Mayer Pictures Inc. All Rights Reserved.

Page 45:   Photograph by Neal Preston for the motion picture *Almost Famous* © 2000 DreamWorks L.L.C. and Columbia Pictures.

Page 47:   *Love Actually*, 2003. Courtesy of Universal Pictures.

Page 49:   *Two Weeks Notice* ©2002 Warner Bros. Inc. All Rights Reserved.

Page 51:   *Chocolat.* Provided courtesy of Miramax Films.

Page 55:   *Fight Club* ©1999 Twentieth Century Fox, Monarchy Enterprises S.a.r.l. and Regency Entertainment (USA), Inc. All Rights Reserved.

Page 57:   *Ocean's Eleven* © 2001 WV Films II LLC. All Rights Reserved.

Page 59:   *The Core.* © Paramount Pictures. All Rights Reserved.

Page 61:   *Harry Potter and the Sorcerer's Stone* © 2001 Warner Bros., a division of Time Warner Entertainment Company L.P. All Rights Reserved.

Page 63:   *The Haunted Mansion* © Disney Enterprises, Inc. All Rights Reserved.

Page 65:   *The Mask of Zorro* ©1998 TriStar Pictures, Inc. All Rights Reserved. Courtesy of TriStar Pictures.

Page 67:   *Unfaithful* ©2002 Twentieth Century Fox, Monarchy Enterprises S.a.r.l. and Regency Entertainment (USA), Inc. All Rights Reserved.

Page 69:   *Runaway Jury* ©2003 Twentieth Century Fox, Monarchy Enterprises S.a.r.l. and Regency Entertainment (USA), Inc. All Rights Reserved.

Page 71:   *Nicholas Nickleby* ©2002 Metro-Goldwyn-Mayer Pictures Inc. All Rights Reserved.

Page 73:   *Blues Brothers 2000*, 1998. Courtesy of Universal Pictures.

Page 75:   *Down with Love* ©2003 Twentieth Century Fox, Monarchy Enterprises S.a.r.l. and Regency Entertainment (USA), Inc. All Rights Reserved.

Page 77:   *Ararat*, Copyright 2002, Serendipity Point Films Inc., All rights reserved courtesy of Serendipity Point Films Inc.

Page 79:   *How to Lose a Guy in 10 Days.* © Paramount Pictures. All Rights Reserved.

Page 81:   *William Shakespeare's A Midsummer Night's Dream* ©1999 Twentieth Century Fox. All Rights Reserved.

Page 83:   *Shanghai Noon* © 2000 Spyglass Entertainment Group, LP. All Rights Reserved.

Page 85:   *102 Dalmatians* © Disney Enterprises, Inc. All Rights Reserved.

Page 87:   *Gangs of New York.* Provided courtesy of Miramax Films.

Page 89:   *Tuck Everlasting* © Disney Enterprises, Inc. All Rights Reserved.

Page 91:   Photograph by Andrew Cooper for the motion picture *The Time Machine* © 2000 DreamWorks L.L.C. and Warner Bros.

Page 93:   *Pirates of the Caribbean: The Curse of the Black Pearl* © Disney Enterprises, Inc. & Jerry Bruckheimer, Inc. All Rights Reserved.

Page 95:   *Cold Mountain.* Provided courtesy of Miramax Films.

Page 97:   *Ronin* ©1998 Metro-Goldwyn-Mayer Pictures Inc. All Rights Reserved.

Page 99:   *Dr. Seuss' How the Grinch Stole Christmas*, 2000. Courtesy of Universal Pictures.

Page 101:   *Extreme Ops.* © Paramount Pictures. All Rights Reserved.

Page 103:   *Elf.* Copyright 2003, New line Productions, Inc. All Rights Reserved. Still appears courtesy of New Line Productions, Inc.

Page 105:   *Frida.* Provided courtesy of Miramax Films.

Page 107:   *Quills* ©2000 Twentieth Century Fox. All Rights Reserved.

Page 109:   Photograph by Francois Duhamel for the motion picture *Road to Perdition* © 2000 DreamWorks L.L.C. and 20th Century Fox

Page 111:   *A Mighty Wind* © 2003 Castle Rock Entertainment. All Rights Reserved.

Page 113:   Photograph by Jaap Buitendijk for the motion picture *Gladiator* © 2000 DreamWorks L.L.C. and Universal Pictures.

Page 115:   *Intolerable Cruelty*, 2003. Courtesy of Universal Pictures.

Published on the occasion of the exhibition
"Fifty Designers/Fifty Costumes: Concept to Character"

at the Galleries of
The Academy of Motion Picture Arts and Sciences
Beverly Hills, California
September 10 – December 5, 2004

Presented in association with the Costume Designers Guild

Exhibition Committee:
Jeffrey Kurland
Deborah Nadoolman Landis
Judianna Makovsky

Costume Designer interviews conducted and edited by
Deborah Nadoolman Landis

Curated and Edited for the Academy by Ellen M. Harrington

Catalogue Design: Jaeger Smith | Los Angeles
Project Coordinator: David McLain
Graphic Art Production: Brett Davidson
Copy Editor: Maryrose McMahon

Copyright © 2004. All rights reserved.
Academy of Motion Picture Arts and Sciences
8949 Wilshire Blvd., Beverly Hills, CA 90211

ISBN # 0-942102-46-0